ENDORSEMENTS

"What a fascinating look into the lives of sixteen very different human beings, who all happen to have made America their new home. How lucky we are to live in a country where this is possible! From the fun stuff like Twinkies and flashlights to the serious stuff like racism and loneliness, this collection is a beautiful and humane illumination of today's immigration experience. A much needed balm for the often too jagged conversation around this huge issue."

Maeve Higgins, Comedian and host of the hit immigration podcast, Maeve in America: Immigration IRL

This book made me relive my own experience when I came to the US when I was 13 years old. The world was a big place back then and the US was a world away for a young guy like me.

Were the cars really as big as they were on TV? Were the buildings as tall as well? What was that, McDonald's? That didn't exist back then in my country. All these overwhelming impressions can be found in this book. Definitely worth a read!

Chris is Managing Director of Culture Matters. He improves the cultural competence of people who work internationally.

https://culturematters.com

Published by Motivational Press, Inc.
1777 Aurora Road
Melbourne, Florida, 32935
www.MotivationalPress.com

ISBN: 978-1-62865-552-0

AMERICA
DECONSTRUCTED

CHAITHANYA SOHAN

AND

SHAIMA ADIN

CONTENTS

Acknowledgements

"I long, as does every human being,
to be at home wherever I find myself."

-Maya Angelou

For every living thing that has helped, challenged, inspired and motivated us – thank you!

For every person who walked a foreign land and made it home, for everyone who weathered the storm and weaved their dream - this is *your* story.

America Deconstructed began as a dream which was weaved into reality by our amazing protagonists, who so willingly shared their life with us. Thank you does not quantify our gratitude to each of these people without whom America Deconstructed would never have been possible. Thank you Naseer, Parag, Myra, JC, Roselin, Azim, Sam, Benedict, Liti, Francisco, Ifeyinwa & Chidiebere, Lisian, Molly and Jose for sharing your life with us.

We have tortured you through the journey of this book and you have been patient the entire way. To our families, spouses and kids - thank you for taking this journey with us.

This book is dedicated to all those who dare to take on a different journey. And to my mom, Najiba Adin, who took the first step. - Shaima Adin

I am what I am because you walked the world holding me. You will always be my strength, the reason I am and my forever hero. I miss you Acha (V.P. Sohan), every second of the day!

- Chaithanya Sohan

FOREWORD

By Paul Varghese

Standup Comedian, Television and Radio Personality

YOU DON'T HAVE TO BE an immigrant or related to immigrants to understand this collection of stories. We've all felt like an outsider-looking-in at some point in our lives. Some of us spend our whole lives dealing with it and some of us just briefly. But the key is to take that awkwardness and mold it into perspective.

I moved out of my parents' house right before I went to college. It was the first time I lived on my own and from that day forward, my mom never answered a phone call from me the same way again.

HELLO was now replaced with DID YOU EAT.

That's been my mom's primary concern any time I call her or visit her, ever since: DID I EAT.

It's been the first question out of her mouth to open any conversation with me for over 20 years and counting. It trumps HOW HAVE YOU BEEN and WHAT'S THAT GROWTH ON YOUR NECK.

"DID YOU EAT?"

I could walk in to her house with noodles on my chin, a fresh ketchup stain on my shirt, chomping on an onion and she'd still ask DID YOU EAT?

Because it's never been about actually eating. It's much bigger than that. DID YOU EAT can mean a variety of things: DON'T FORGET ABOUT ME, I MISS YOU, I LOVE YOU

I used to think I was deprived because all of my American friends' parents would say I LOVE YOU to them. But then I looked at what my American friends' parents cooked for them to eat: corn on the cob, mashed potatoes, and cold-cut sandwiches - Foods that took less than 30 minutes to make. A lot of times, they even ordered delivery or went out to eat. My parents never ordered delivery. My dad didn't want strangers knowing where we lived. And if we ever did go out to eat, it was for my mom's birthday because it was the only time she didn't have to cook. And she always wanted to go to Indian restaurants and I never understood why. Because every single time she would take one taste of any food at any Indian restaurant, she'd always say I CAN MAKE THIS BETTER

My parents even grew all the vegetables they used to cook with in their backyard. They didn't grow anything back there for decoration. If they were growing it, they were eating it. It could be a bed full of roses; someway-somehow it's going to end up in some curry:

"Kids, I made daffodil samosas!"

"Mom, there's a bee in it."

"That means it's honey-sweet."

The most obvious difference with my American friend's meals and my parents' meals was in how they named them. The names of the American dishes always had the ingredients listed in it

"This is a garlic lemon pepper chicken."

You know exactly how to make it: garlic, lemon, pepper, and chicken

If my mom named her dishes after the ingredients listed in it, we wouldn't have time to eat

"This is a garlic, ginger, cumin, coriander, onion, turmeric, salt, red pepper, black pepper, Dr. Pepper .."

All those hours tending to the garden and adding ingredients just to create this decadent meal every single night. That's what unconditional love is. That's how they showed it.

I didn't realize any of this until years later.

Being born and raised in the United States, you have this Americanized standard of how your family is supposed to act. I remember the first time I saw one of my Indian friend's dad say I LOVE YOU, I thought to myself "Is his dad dying?" Growing up, I thought I wanted that and that I needed that.

Now as an adult, I realize I didn't and I don't.

It's just words.

I throw around the word LOVE all the time.

From "I LOVE this song" to "I LOVE breakfast burritos".

The true definition of love is in the actions.

My parents have been there for me more than anyone else has and should ever be for someone.

I'm lucky.

I'm grateful.

And the next time I go to visit my mom's house and she opens the door in her denim moo-moo with plastic gloves on her hands so she doesn't get the "fish smell" on them when she's cutting it, and she answers the door with DID YOU EAT

I'll reply with "I LOVE YOU, TOO."

An Alien In America!

"**A**RE YOU READY TO LEAVE?" she asked me, walking out of her room. I was enamored by the microwave in our kitchen and had been staring at it for minutes now. I turned around. I knew the voice, but did not recognize the person standing in front of me. The lady whose sari-clad figure had been part of my childhood years now stood in pants and a t-shirt. The image of her in pants signaled the end of the life I knew in a lot of ways. I composed myself and calmed my whirlwind of emotions. It was 9:30am on a warm July morning when my mom and I walked out of the hotel and into the deserted streets of Pleasanton. A male voice called out, "Hello Ladies," as we walked. We did not dare turn around or respond, but walked faster. His presence was still behind us and from the corner of my eye, I could see his tall frame. I told my mom he looked tall and dark. We turned into the 7-Eleven parking lot when the man overtook us. He stood in front of us blocking our entrance to the store. I did not know what my options were. We were a few hours into our new life in America and, with no cell phone on us, we were clueless on what our options were. Less than 24 hours in the United States of America and I feared for both our lives.

Twenty-four hours prior, I was sitting on an Eva Airlines flight watching the sun set. As the stewardess announced our descent upon San Francisco, I remember seeing the skyline. The orange and yellow sunset against the San Francisco skyline signaled the beginning of a new life. As I sat there watching nature's display, I was reminded of a movie

I watched a few years back titled Pardes ("Foreign" in Hindi). The San Francisco skyline looked exactly like the skyline from the movie.

After a grueling few hours clearing customs and immigrations, I was officially welcomed into America with an alien number. I stood waiting for my baggage and realized I had successfully made the journey I had dreaded for the past few months. Unlike most immigrants, who plan their trip to America for years or decades, I was given few months notice. My parent was suddenly transferred from their Indian office to America and, within months, I knew I was immigrating to America after my 12th grade. I resisted the move, insisting I complete my college in India. Since I was in tenth grade, I had made plans of what my college life in India would entail. My friends and I were going to ditch classes to watch movies, have boyfriends, and do everything that college life in India guaranteed. Standing in the San Francisco airport made the move concrete and I combated a gamut of emotions. I felt all my dreams of college life shatter and I missed my family and friends back in India. I always wanted to attend graduate school in America or UK. But at eighteen years of age, I stood outside San Francisco airport and knew everything was happening too soon.

But, as I walked through the airport to our car, the fear and apprehension was slowly replaced by excitement. I was enamored by everything - from the elevators to the parking garage. I was excited to finally reach our car, as I was about to see what America was really like. Everything around me was new. I was ready for America. The car drove through the parking garage exit and I looked around in amazement. Even the parking garage looked nothing like the ones back in India. We entered the freeway. I wasn't aware of what a freeway would be like. It felt like a real life NASCAR race - cars overtaking one another. My hand gripped the handle as cars zoomed by. The end of the NASCAR race was a relief, especially after a twenty-three hour flight. Our hotel was located in Pleasanton, California, in a strip mall. There were several shops, restaurants, and a movie theater. We were given a hotel suite with a kitchen and two bedrooms by my parent's office. I spent all night watching people throng the mall as I combated my jetlag and excitement. I could not wait for the next morning to begin my American adventure.

The previous twenty-four hours flashed before my eyes. It was morning and I was ready to begin my new life. When we left our hotel, I felt safe knowing I was in America. But, staring at the man who cornered us, I cursed myself for letting my guard down. The six-foot-tall, African American man who followed us to 7-Eleven was smiling. My mom and I held hands and huddled closer. We were scared. He seemed satisfied to have finally cornered his prey. The man said with glee, "Y'all are pretty. Where are y'all from?" I knew I had problems understanding American English, so I wondered if he really just called us pretty. Why would he do that before hurting us? "India," I responded coyly. "You ladies have a good day," he said and, with that, he walked into 7-Eleven. We stood there shocked, but were even more appalled that he called us pretty. He could have called us Angelina Jolie and we would have still been offended. In India, men never compliment women directly. Usually they speak incognito around them. We decided to skip going into 7-Eleven, just in case he tried to talk to us again.

I reached America on July 12, 2001. Most colleges begin reviewing transcripts in May and have a decision for students by July. Since I missed the deadline, I was forced to stay home for six months and start college during the spring semester. I used those six months to acquaint myself with America. We rented an apartment and no longer stayed in a hotel, which gave us an actual address and sense of normalcy. Those six months were also used in attempt to return to India for college. I threw tantrums and acted depressed for a while, but realized my parents were never going to send me back. Eventually I caved in and accepted my new life. My mom and I spent our days walking to the nearby Walmart, going to parks, and renting Indian movies from the Indian grocery store. Since we did not have a car or know how to drive, we walked everywhere. Slowly we were regaining our confidence and getting used to the American ways. We bought a car as soon as one of us had a license. Six months had already gone by.

The day I had dreamed about since seventh grade was nearing - I was officially going to be a college student. A week before classes begun I was excited, but as the day neared it morphed into gut wrenching fear. It got to the point that I could not sleep at night, so my mom offered to come with me on my first day. I had it all planned out. I was going to wear my best jeans, t-shirt, and sweatshirt for college. We took two buses and a train to San Jose State University. I was still feeling fairly confident until I walked through the gates of San Jose State University. Instantly I knew I was underdressed. I was a tomboy who loved wearing baggy clothes. I wore jeans two sizes bigger than me and my sweatshirt hung loose on my body. I also had very short and boyish haircut. As much as I was shocked by the different fashions around me, I had bigger problems to deal with. I stared at the map in my hands with stars on different buildings. Those were the buildings I had classes in, but I had no idea how to get to them. I had never used a map to navigate in my life. During our freshmen orientation we were given a campus map. I had marked the various buildings for my classes the night before. I stood near San Jose State University entrance with no idea how to reach any of the buildings. Eventually, after making several wrong turns, I reached the engineering building for my first class almost 20 minutes late. I was just in time for attendance and I knew I would be called any minute. After a few names, the professor paused in brief silence, staring at his sheet with a baffled look. He stuttered, paused, and looked confused as he called me by my last name. He asked how to pronounce my first name. When I told him Chai-tanya, he exclaimed how easy it was. This incident followed me throughout the day and for most of my college life. I obliged every time someone looked confused by my name. I wore my full name with pride and refused to shorten it until my senior year happened. My teammates and I were spending summer working with a professor on a project and were done for the day. As we walked down the hallway, I heard someone say "Shit-tanya" instead. I did a double take, but he really did call me Shit-tanya. I shortened my name to Chai that instant, hoping I would never be called Shit-tanya again. In spite of shortening my name, I still get called Chi, Kai, Che, etc. People often tell me Chai means tea in their country. I stop myself from telling them chai originated in my country and let them have their moment. I have my moment every time I visit Starbucks with Chai latte named after me - or so I want to believe.

Before I could start college, I had to decide on the classes for the semester. I was clueless, so I followed the four-year plan that was given during orientation. The plan included math, general engineering, English and public speaking. I had no idea what public speaking entailed, but I took it as instructed in the four-year plan. During my introductory English class, we were asked to introduce ourselves. My introduction included the country I was from and how long I had lived here. As soon as the class ended, one of my classmates stopped me and said, "You must feel really lucky to have bathrooms now. I have watched documentaries of people taking showers on the street in India." He stood there watching my expression change from confusion to anger while I composed myself enough to explain how I grew up having bathrooms.

I was confident in my math and English skills, but not so sure about public speaking. I walked into my public speaking class on my very first day at San Jose State University. The professor began briefing us on what we would need to do in order to get an A. "You will need to prepare and present three speeches on various topics that are assigned to you," he said. I was sure I heard it wrong. I cleared my ears and asked the person sitting next to me if the professor actually said three speeches. I have been on stage since I was three years old and have emceed several events in India. I was used to presenting in front of a large crowd. But this was America. As I looked around the class and saw different ethnicities of people around, I felt my confidence disappear. I knew I was in trouble when the professor said the first speech was due in two weeks and it had to be on a topic that represented us ethnically. I did my first speech on henna (Indian artwork tattoo). I stayed up all night presenting my speech in front of the mirror. I was ready, but as I reached the stage, my legs began vibrating. I was so nervous that the professor asked for a podium to ease my stress. I was still shaking behind the podium. I had to give three speeches for my public speaking class and I shook my way through all three of them.

I have often been complimented on my English speaking skills. People ask me if I learned to speak English after I came to America. Initially, I would tell them we learned English in school and listened to Backstreet Boys and Britney Spears like the rest of the world, but now I politely offer thanks. In spite of speaking good English, I did not realize there was a big difference between British and American English beyond the accents. Oblivious to the differences, I once told my friend I had called him the day before but his phone was engaged. He laughed while I stood there baffled. I was clueless until he asked me engaged to whom. I forgot all about it until he asked me one day if he could borrow my pen because his pen was engaged. As ridiculous as this might sound, engaged is only used for the phone in India.

I have always been an introvert and extremely shy. In spite of being a popular girl in my high school, I have always had trouble in big groups and cannot eat in front of strangers. The social scene in American colleges warrants eating out with people and I constantly shied away from it. I was completely wary of the dating scene when I first started college. When guys asked for my number, I gave it to them even when I wasn't attracted to them. It took me months before I realized asking my phone number had nothing to do with studying or even the classes we took. One of the guys who eventually became my friend asked me out to lunch and dinner for months. I always evaded him, saying my mom cooked for me or I wasn't hungry. Eventually he asked me out to a coffee at Starbucks, which I could not refuse. I walked into Starbucks and stared at the menu on the wall. I had no idea what Cappuccino and Frappuccino was, so I ordered coffee. It was my first drink order in America. I expected my coffee to have milk and sugar like it did in India, but what I received was black coffee. My date showed me to the milk section. I was confused at the options I had to choose from. I had no idea what 1% milk, non-fat and 2% meant, so I decided to skip milk. I added two packets of sugar, assuming one packet equated to a teaspoon. I excitedly took a sip of my coffee. It was bitter. The two packets of sugar disappeared in the black hole in my cup. I stalled drinking the coffee until our bus arrived and gladly threw it away on the pretense that it wasn't allowed on the bus. Eating out has also been extremely challenging for me and it took me several years before I learned to deal with it. Initially we only ate fast foods, such as burgers and pizza. When we did go out to sit down restaurants, I watched my parents and emulated how they used the fork and knife. In spite of coming from a multicultural background, I could never comprehend how to use a fork and knife. I always felt very anxious when the waitress chanted the options. Until I graduated from college, my parents ordered my food whenever we went out to eat.

When I first moved to America, my confidence was shaken up. I lacked confidence to do things I knew I was good at. Basketball happened to be one such activity. I had been in love with basketball since I was ten years old. I played at the state level in India and had a scholarship to play basketball in college. I idolized Michael Jordan and Magic Johnson and wore my Chicago Bulls jersey with élan. I dreamed of playing in the NBA. During my freshman year in college, I found out San Jose State University was having basketball tryouts for the freshmen. I was excited and reached the tryouts an hour early. With time, the other girls walked in. Most of them were African American and they seemed to know one another. I sat in the corner and watched the girls chat back and forth. My nerves kicked in and eventually turned to fear. I knew I was good at basketball, but sitting in that corner I started doubting my skills. Eventually, in spite of pep talking to myself, I caved and ran out before I could ever try out. Basketball continues to enthrall me, but my dream to be a professional player remains unfulfilled.

Four years at San Jose State University changed me as a person. I was an introverted tomboy when I first walked into college. I wore baggy jeans, t-shirts, and sweatshirts with my boyish hair. While I still believe I rocked my look, I've changed to become more acceptable to America's standards. In those four years at college, my jeans got tighter, my t-shirts morphed into fashionable tops, and the sweatshirts evolved into cardigans. It took almost two years of a slow progression for my appearance to change. In my own way, I learned to balance being myself with the American standard. My hair has grown, but I refuse to get bangs. My earrings continue to be studs and I refuse to conform to the chandelier-wearing Indian American model. I might have changed on the outside, but deep down I am the same Indian girl who boarded the plane on that July day. I love my Indian food, Bollywood music, and Shahrukh Khan (an Indian actor) continues to make my heart flutter.

When my family and I went to the consulate to get my US visa, the officer swore I would marry a US citizen. I shrugged it off, insisting I had a prototype for my man. He would be tall, tan, and handsome with the quintessential Indian haircut. In 2003, I met a curly haired African

American boy in my computer engineering class who ended up being unlike anyone I had met. We exchanged hi and bye for little over a year. One day I decided to ditch my class and gave him my phone number, so he could call me if there was a quiz. The calls that followed did not include a quiz, but a friendship that eventually turned into romance. In 2008, we got married in an Indian-American fusion wedding. I had lived in America for over seven years at this point and was convinced my cultural differences were behind me. Little did I know being married to an American would have it's own challenges culturally. Even after five years of friendship, my husband still chuckles when I say calcium or aluminum with a British accent. In America, calcium is pronounced as cal-c-um while the British pronunciation is cal-cheum. A few years into our marriage, I told my husband about a coworker who met with an accident. He started laughing, saying they had an accident, not met with an accident. With him, I live a cultural mix-masala every day.

A few months into our marriage, I was invited to a summer barbeque at his aunt's house. I had not met his extended family until then. It was louder than I expected. I was welcomed by a slew of high-pitched voices, introducing themselves as family. I was the first Indian girl in their family and I tried to be the best ambassador of my culture. I tasted my first peach cobbler and realized it was an acquired taste. While I love my banana puddings and carrot cake, I would rather have my gulab jamun and jalebi (both Indian desserts) any day. In the eight years we have been married, I have also introduced Indian food to my extended family. In 2014, I made my famous Indian spicy chicken for a Thanksgiving potluck. My in-laws opened the lid of the container and felt the radiating heat from the chili powder. As they contemplated if they should taste it, they saw my husband eating it with much ease in the corner. They were shocked until one of his cousins said, "What did y'all expect? He is married to an Indian girl!"

I visited India in 2009 after eight years in America. This was my first visit back home and my husband's first visit to India. My family pampered him by being at his beck and call. They ensured he was comfortable by adding ketchup to Indian dishes to reduce the spice. Wherever we went, people tried to ease him into the Indian ways. He played American football since school and is built like American football players. Sales women at stores insisted on helping him with clothes as they wondered why a football player was built like him. They asked him if he was related to Mohammed Ali because of his body type. In India, football was soccer and they had no idea about American football. Neighbors told him they loved President Obama, while my husband wondered why they were talking about the President to him. In India, my husband was related to President Obama, Mohammed Ali, and Will Smith. In short, it was his big Indian adventure and my homecoming.

The initial years in America were extremely hard. I came here on an H4 dependent visa and was not allowed to work. My Indian parents did not want me to work. Instead they wanted me to concentrate on my studies. At college, my friends often teased me for being lazy and not working. In order to combat that, I started volunteering for organizations without pay. It allowed me to tell people I worked in spite of not being paid. When I left India for America, I told my friends I would visit them every few years. It took me eight years before I went back to India. My parents did not want me to go back on a visa, just in case the US consulate did not let me return back. I waited until I got my green card to visit India. I was homesick every second of those eight years. America was home, but it never felt like home.

It's been fifteen years since I landed in America. I was seventeen then. Since that day, I have received two engineering degrees and married my husband. Yet, every time I look at the mirror, I see the seventeen-year-old me looking back in the reflection. America has given me everything

- education, marriage, career, and a fairly luxurious life. Yet, I yearn for the simplicity of life back home. I miss drinking tea to the monsoon, the talks I had with my grandmother each evening, my friends who visited me with no prior notice, and the childish banter that always followed those visits. The hardest aspect of my American life has been the loneliness I feel everyday living here. In spite of having family here, America has never felt like home.

As I walked out of Chennai airport on that visit to India, I realized I was home. The air felt familiar, the smells and sounds echoed my childhood. All my life, I have been told home is where your family is. It's not entirely right. I met my friends after eight years and I was nervous, wondering how the time could have changed our friendship. I knew how stupid I was when I met my friends. It seemed like time had stood still. It felt like I had never left India. The conversations flowed as we walked through streets, holding hands like we did in school. For the first time in eight years, I felt the sense of belonging I had yearned for in years. During those three weeks in India, I realized my physical address could be anywhere in the world, but my home would forever be India.

Azim Karimi Is a Happy Man

I DID NOT HAVE A WATCH indicating the time. I could not see any light enter the crevices of the wall signaling night and day. I could not remember how many days I had been sitting in this dark cell. Was it a day or had it been years? I didn't know, but it felt like eons. I had nothing to do but ponder on this trivial information. Hope diminished with every second I spent in that small cell. It felt like the day before I was working as a technician at the Afghan University. I only saw people when I was beaten and tortured by the guards. Each time I saw one of them walk into my cell, I knew what followed. I was scared and nervous. Thoughts of never walking free clouded my thoughts.

My life had been headed in the right direction. I attended Afghan Institute of Technology, established by the Americans in Kabul. Upon graduation, I worked as a technician in the College of Engineering at the Afghan University. Three years passed as a technician, when one day I was told I was admitted to the university for engineering. I was beyond happy knowing I was going to university. Afghanistan was under the communist regime at that time and they were opposed to Afghans receiving education from the Americans. As more Afghans began attending the universities and colleges run by Americans, things started going south. Things got so bad that 48 American professors and staff members at the education institutions were ordered to leave the country immediately. The people who attended the institutions, Afghans who taught in these institutions, or those affiliated were all considered communist targets. I remember I had stayed up late studying for my midterm exams the night before. I was a sophomore. I had heard they were arresting people around the city who were affiliated with Americans. As I walked through my university gate, I saw several military trucks full of men in uniforms pull in to the university parking lot. The men jumped out of the trucks loaded with arms and ammunition. There were several of them. I was scared, but hopeful I might not be arrested or taken away. All that changed in minutes when one of my professors asked me to report to the Dean's office. I was trembling with fear and knew I was in trouble. As I walked into the Dean's office, I saw uniformed men with guns standing around. "We will be taking him outside for questioning," one of the men said. I hoped someone would rescue me from the situation, but it never happened. I followed the men outside.

"Is your name Azim?" they asked. I stood there worried. I wanted to deny, but I knew I would be in greater trouble for lying. I nodded my head. "Are there any other Azims in this university?" I told them I wasn't sure and they would have to ask admissions for that information. I saw a silver lining and was hopeful there might be another Azim somewhere who would free me. But the silver lining melted away as the uniformed guy chose to ignore me. He said he was taking me for interrogation. Once we reached the car, I asked if I could lock the lab before going. He denied my request. I insisted on going, at which point he pointed the gun under his jacket at me and told me to do as I was instructed. I knew if I disobeyed I might be dead. I got in the car fearing for my life. I knew if I did survive the interrogation, my father would rescue me out of anywhere. My father retired from the military and could use his contacts to get me out.

I ran the scenario leading to my arrest million times while I sat in my cell. I wondered what could have happened if the guard had chosen to check for other Azims. But he didn't and there were only three outcomes for my situation: I could end up in prison, go to a correction facility, or be executed. I did not know if one was better than the other. It felt like the end of the road for me – I wondered if I was ever going to get out of there. One fine day I heard the cell gate open and the guard said, "Azim, let's go." I was told I had been in jail for two weeks. Those two weeks felt like a lifetime. My dad's friend, who was part of the communist party, called his contacts to get me out of jail. They let me go on one condition - I had to sign a release form that prevented me from talking about the beating and torture I endured in those two weeks.

Those two weeks in jail had a deep impact on my life. The bruises healed with time, the scars began to fade, but the torture I faced in jail continued to haunt me for years to come. I could not tell anyone about those two weeks. I continued to work at the university, pretending like everything was normal. I knew in my heart things were far from normal. I knew I had to leave Afghanistan as soon as possible. My stint in jail made me a possible suspect for the rest of my life. Each day I feared I would be picked up again as a suspect for interrogation. Each day I had a target on my back. My fears came true when one of my friends informed me of the undercover cops who were looking for me at the university. He told the cops I wasn't there and warned me they were possibly going to my house. "No matter where you go, make sure you don't go home," my friend warned me. I rode my bike as fast as I could to my relatives' house. I asked them to inform my parents about the situation. As I waited for the tensions to subside, I was told the cops mistook my uncle for me and took him for interrogation. During interrogation they realized they had the wrong guy and released him. I had to leave Afghanistan as soon as possible if I wanted to be a free man. After days of planning, my relatives bought me a ticket to Khost, a bordering province to Pakistan. I would then cross Pakistan, although the plan did not detail how I was going to cross Pakistan. I left Kabul for Khost without meeting my parents or saying farewell to the people I was closest to.

I reached Khost as planned. Instantly I realized there was more chaos in Khost than in Kabul. The government forces and freedom fighters (Mujahedeen) that wanted to rid Afghanistan of the Russian influences were fighting amidst each other. The situation was very bad. I did not know how I was going to cross the border into Pakistan. My friend's uncle told me the only way to cross the border was to walk the distance by foot. On a cold morning when the horizon was dark, we began our journey towards the high mountains bordering Pakistan. We walked for hours, with the initial three hours being the most terrifying. There were moments when we feared getting shot. After three hours of looking over our shoulders, we crossed the rivers and were finally safe from government forces. It took three days before we reached the border. During those three days, the local villagers and mosques on our path provided food and shelter for us. The Mujahedeen's helped us tremendously as well. The Mujahedeen's were American allies fighting against the communist government.

Finally after days, I reached Peshawar, Pakistan, with $1000 in my pocket. I met several other Afghan refugees who were going to Germany and other European countries. My friend helped me get a passport for $500 and a ticket to United Kingdom for $500. I flew to Karachi from Peshawar to board my flight to Germany the next day. The plan was to reach United Kingdom through Germany and France. I arrived at the airport for my flight to Germany and was first in line at the check-in counter. The guy looked at my passport and said, "Oh, you are Afghan?" I did not know what that meant but what followed crushed me. He said, "Sorry, Afghans cannot go to Germany without a visa." I was even more disappointed when I found out the night before they received a notice from Germany stating Afghans would need a visa to enter Germany going forward. The guy at the check-in counter asked me to go to the German embassy to get my visa. I went to the German embassy and filled out an application for my visa. Days turned to months as the wait continued for my visa. I was tired of waiting. One morning I decided to go to the airport again. I went to the counter, showed them my passport and ticket. The guy asked me of my intended destination. I told him United Kingdom and wondered what was going to happen. Lady Luck smiled on me finally as he stamped my passport. I walked to my flight and thought I was dreaming – I wanted to board my flight before I woke up.

My final destination was United Kingdom, but I intended to stay in Germany during my layover. Upon reaching Germany I filed for political asylum, which allowed me to stay in Germany until my case was processed. The German system was completely different than what I was used to. They required thirteen years of high school as opposed to Afghanistan. Everyone spoke German. Within my first few days, I realized I would have to learn the language if I wanted to stay there.

I was very discouraged by my prospects in Germany, and called my professors in Afghanistan for help. They suggested I apply for political asylum in the United States of America, so I applied at the American embassy. As soon as I applied for the US visa, my political asylum in Germany was accepted as well. While waiting for my American visa, I applied for jobs in Germany. I knew it would be difficult, but I was educated and could speak English - I was confident I could survive in Germany. Reality turned out to be very different. I doubted if I would ever learn German. I had no money or a job to support my stay in Germany. A month after I was accepted in Germany, I received my American visa. I was beyond excited to go to the United States of America.

When I first landed in Germany, I was looking forward to a new beginning. In addition to my financial and language problems, people were not very nice to foreigners like me. People who didn't look white were treated like second-class citizens. While each day in Germany was a challenge, I also received a beautiful gift in the form of my first wife.

She came to Germany seeking asylum like I did. We did not know what America would be like, but we packed our bags and began our new journey. I left Germany as a married man to begin a new life in America. Sitting on the flight to America, I decided I wanted to continue my education while working. I knew it was going to be difficult, but treading difficult paths was my forte.

The year was 1981. We landed in New York City. The tall and beautiful New York skyline instantly welcomed us. I was told I would be living 50 miles away from capital, which I assumed was Washington D.C. I imagined Washington D.C. to be like New York, or even more beautiful because it was the capital. We were told to board another flight to Kansas. We landed in Wichita, Kansas, where we met the family who would help us settle in America. They greeted us and drove us to our final destination. I looked around hoping for the tall and beautiful American skyline I imagined. I noticed Kansas was nothing like New York or Washington D.C. I kept looking for tall buildings, but we continued to drive away from any city life I saw around us. The lands turned to farmlands as the roads seemed barren. I was extremely disappointed by my American welcome. We were going to live in the middle of nowhere.

I thought I was going to live in one of those big cities in America, but ended up living in a small town with a population of about 10,000 people. We were among the few immigrant families in our city and were treated like celebrities. I noticed people in America were nicer than Germany. Everyone who visited us wanted to learn about our culture and food. Even the local newspapers met us hoping to run an article about me in their newspaper. I felt like a celebrity for the first time in my life. I spoke good English, which made communication easy. We were invited to speak at various churches, schools, and other institutions about Afghan culture. The next morning I was surprised to find my picture in the newspaper titled "Azim Karimi Is a Happy Man."

I was a local celebrity and everyone knew about me. I even received a letter from the governor and senator welcoming me to Kansas. The governor offered his help if I needed anything. While I was enjoying my stardom in Kansas, I knew I wanted to build a life in America. I decided to attend Kansas State. I remembered the governor's offer and wrote a letter asking if he could help me with my admission and fees at Kansas State. I was very new to the American system and was completely unaware of the financial aid availability. I waited to hear back from the governor, but ended up receiving a big package from Kansas State with all the information regarding the admission and financial aid. The governor's office had directly contacted Kansas State University regarding my admission. I was beyond elated. I walked into college at Kansas State University and felt right at home. I saw similarities between the education system at Kansas State and the University in Afghanistan. The desks and chairs were the same. Many of the textbooks were the same ones I had read in Afghanistan. I was welcomed with open arms in college by my peers. I felt at home in America.

Although I qualified for financial aid, I worked part time to afford a life for my wife and me. My first job was at Dairy Queen in their ice-cream department. I was paid minimum wage of $3.35 an hour. My manager came up to me one day and asked if I could clean the food from under the table which was dropped by one of the customers. I looked at her and could not believe she would request me to clean the floor. I refused to clean the floor. My manager could have fired me, but she allowed me to explain my reasons. I told her I was an educated man and was surprised she would ask me to do something as low as cleaning the floor. I had high self-esteem and believed I should be doing professional work. My manager laughed it off. It did not take long before I realized if I wanted to survive in America I would have to do any work I was offered. With that revelation, I started doing jobs such as painting people's homes, driving a taxi at night, and working in construction while attending school during the day. The taxi allowed me to complete my homework in the car during downtimes. I would work until 6am, sleep for three hours, and then attend classes at 9am.

The days when I worked and went to school were hard on me physically. The hard work began paying off as I began bringing my entire family to the United States, one person at a time. My family had immigrated to Pakistan by then, making the process easier. The senator in Kansas helped with my family moving here, and the immigration process was easier too. Initially my older brothers were denied their visas. The senator pulled strings at the American Embassy in Pakistan and my brothers joined us in the US soon after. America in the 1980's was very different than what it is today. The rent was cheap. I remember paying $100 for a good size apartment. I was able to do a lot with my minimum wage salary.

Years passed by and before I knew it, I was graduating from Kansas State University in December 1986. It was a big milestone in our lives. I had worked hard for this day. I started looking for jobs, but Kansas did not have opportunities for electrical engineers. I applied for jobs all over the United States. One of my professors from Kabul University had moved to California in 1986. He asked me to visit him and told me about the opportunities California offered for technical majors. I decided to visit him in the Bay Area for a month. I was browsing through the San Jose Mercury newspaper during my visit when I noticed there were three pages of opportunities for engineers. I decided then to move to California. I went back to Kansas, packed everything, bid adieu to friends, and moved to Bay Area in July 1987. While there were several opportunities for engineers in California, they required experience, which a new graduate did not possess. I remember interviewing at a company where the person told me I did not have enough experience for the job I applied to. I had heard it several times already and I was frustrated so I asked him, "Where do they sell experience for me to purchase? Will Walmart sell experience to a new graduate like me?" Finally, I started working as a technician. I did that for six months before I was offered a position as an R&D Engineer in Sunnyvale, at one of their branches. Life started moving in the right direction. I received promotions and, with time, I started climbing the corporate ladder.

I have lived in America for thirty-four years now and have witnessed the changing times. I have seen things change for the worse in the years I have lived here. I remember getting paid $3.35 an hour and raising a family with it. I could afford a normal living with the money I was getting paid then, but now a middle-class income is not enough to survive in America. Everything has become about money and business here. It was easier to make it in America thirty years back than it is now. The American system and party affiliations of Democrats versus Republicans have become an issue in this country. If one party wants to do something good for the people here, the other party will oppose just because it is coming from the opposing side. There is no bipartisan work being done here. This is supposed to be the greatest country on Earth - I witnessed its greatness when I first came here, but now it is changing for the worse. I still believe things can revert back to how it used to be and improve for the better.

I always tried to stay connected to my culture. I have always been very excited to introduce my culture to the West. I remember the day I arrived in Kansas like it was yesterday. I had just arrived from Germany, where I had rarely felt welcome. Kansas bowled me over with how friendly everyone was. I felt very welcome in Kansas. I drove for hours to see Afghan families that lived in different corners of Kansas. I tried to introduce my culture to my children as much as I could. I feel proud every time I see my children enjoy Afghan food. I feel overwhelming emotions knowing my children can read and write in our native language. I feel pride seeing them wear their culture proudly on their sleeve. I tried very hard to stay connected to my motherland, Afghanistan. I went back to Afghanistan several times after twenty-two years of life in America. Instantly I noticed a different Afghanistan than the one of my childhood. People were different, and were not as friendly as I remembered them to be. I felt the mountains of Afghanistan echoed the tears of warfare, the buildings bore signs of the bloodshed around, and the trees where I spent my childhood years reflected the fears and pain of their surroundings. I was yearning to go back to the Afghanistan of my childhood but when I reached there, I felt I didn't belong. I have been in America for thirty-four years now. I have called this country my own. The country has given me everything I have today and has allowed me to provide for my family. I want to see this country go back to the America I lived in where people were friendlier and trusted each other. There was a sense of community that instantly made America home to an immigrant like me.

I Saw a Ripe Mango I'd Like to Pluck

She is vivacious with a glint of mischief in her eyes. He is silent, calm, and composed. She is taller than most women, well dressed in her skinny jeans and green top with a purse casually hanging on her side. He is tall, casually dressed with a serious aura around him. Together they ooze chemistry. Every time she watched him speak, her eyes sparkled with love. She lazily rested her head against his shoulder, sometimes resting her hand on him and sometimes jokingly taunting him. He had his hand around her protectively, intently watching her as she spoke. Together they made sweet love and music with every word they rhythmically spoke in their Nigerian accent, often stealing glances at each other. Ifeyinwa and Chidiebere flaunted their heritage visually in their movements and words as they chatted about culture, Nigeria, and their life in America.

Glimpse into Nigeria:

Nigeria is in West Africa. We are from the eastern part of Nigeria and called the Igbo people. The southern parts of Nigeria are Christians and the northern parts of Nigeria are Muslims. So Nigeria has 50 percent Christians and 50 percent Muslims. We got our independence from the British in 1960. English is the medium of education in Nigeria because of the British influence. However, Nigeria has 250 different languages, not just dialects. Often you have no idea what the other person is saying because of this. It is the most populous black country in the world, with about 170 million people living there. It is a beautiful place to live in. There are no natural disasters such as earthquakes and volcanoes. It is in the tropical rain forest, so the weather is warm all year round for the most part. People live very organic lifestyles. They grow their vegetables, raise their own chickens, and pretty much everything they eat. Growing up in Nigeria was lots of fun. It was relaxed and the lifestyle was very simple. School fees were nothing in comparison to what we pay in America. The primary and secondary school was practically free. Even college education was very cheap. If we had to compare, we paid probably about $10 in college fees. This was how we grew up in Nigeria back then. Now everything has changed. School and colleges have become expensive because there are more private institutions there. Back when we were in school and college, there were only public institutions. It is the fourth largest oil producing country in the world and is the main source of income for Nigeria.

CHIDIEBERE IN AMERICA:

I came here in August 1995 on a Diversity Immigration Visa called a DV1 lottery. America gives 50,000 visas to people from other countries to come here on practically a green card. The computer randomly chooses the people who would receive the DV1 visa. My dad's friend who visited Nigeria told me about the DV1 visa. He asked me, "Are you interested?" I said sure, why not. On a blank sheet of paper I wrote down my name, date of birth, and address. I was told they were sending the paper to New Hampshire or somewhere. I forgot about it and went about my business. I had recently graduated from college and was working at Michelin Tires when I got a letter saying I won the lottery. I said great, I won the lottery. I went to the consulate with my documents. The next thing I knew, I was coming to the United States of America. In Nigeria, after undergrad everyone serves the government for a year. As soon as I finished serving the government after one year, I came here in August 1995.

Receiving the DV1 visa was exciting, but it was also scary in some ways. I was having fun in Nigeria. I knew the direction my life was headed. When I received my DV1 visa to America, I was faced with several uncertainties. I was worried how I was going to survive in this new place. Besides that, I did not have any expectations about America. It was my first flight, but I was not scared of anything. I entered United States through Minnesota. My uncle, who was in San Jose, arranged my trip to the United States of America. I thought America was small and asked my uncle, "Oh, are you going to pick me up from Minnesota?" My uncle told me no and explained California was very far from Minnesota. I would be taking another flight from Minnesota to San Jose, California. My uncle picked me up from the airport and took me home. They lived in a two-bedroom apartment with four kids. I shared a room with two of the kids. It was rough initially. They had one bathroom for seven people. I was in my twenties and sharing a room with children was not on my agenda. I stayed there for five months and then moved out.

While in Nigeria, I remember people telling me no matter what career you had in Nigeria, when you come to America you have to pay your dues. You have to start from scratch and that's what I did. Three weeks into being in America, I started working at McDonald's during the day flipping burgers and as security during the night. Instantly I realized it would take some adjustments to understand the accents. People spoke very fast here and I often had to ask people to repeat themselves. Within two-to-three months I bought a car. Working at McDonald's was hard work. I was on my feet almost the whole day and with two jobs, I hardly got any rest. While working at McDonald's and the security company, I started applying to other jobs. I had graduated with a Bachelor's in Industrial Chemistry from the University of Nigeria. I had technicians working for me in Nigeria. I had gone from being a supervisor to flipping burgers. When I started applying to jobs here, I decided to apply for managerial positions. Every time I read the job description for a manager, I figured I could do it. One of the companies I applied to called and asked me if I wanted to work as a technician. I accepted the technician position at a semiconductor company and resigned from McDonald's. Two years later, I started my Master's in 1997. Life happened and before I knew it I was looking to get married.

WHEN WE MET:

Ifeyinwa: I met Chidiebere through my sister, who lives in Atlanta with her husband. Her husband was from the same place as Chidiebere. In Nigeria, when men want to get married they can either marry their girlfriend if they have one or they can get recommendations from people they know. They want the best woman, whom they call wife material. They pass on the message that they are looking for a wife. Everyone in the community gives recommendations for the beautiful girls who can cook and are from respectable families for consideration. That was how I was recommended to him. He had some other girls he was checking out. If I had known about the other girls, I would not have stayed in any competition. He never wanted to marry someone that was recommended. He wanted to be introduced to them so he can get to know them, become friends, and then eventually get married.

Chidiebere: I never wanted to get married to someone who was in Nigeria. I wanted to marry someone who was in the United States, had a job, and was doing her own thing. I tried that out and met some girls who were here. I didn't like any of them. Ifeyinwa's brother-in-law (sister's husband) was my friend from Nigeria. Her brother-in-law and I often talked about my marriage situation. After a while, he told me his wife had two sisters who I might want to check out. I said no problem and they sent me their pictures. I took a look at their pictures and decided to call one of them.

Ifeyinwa: (Interrupting) He looked at the two pictures and thought my sister was finer (better looking) than I was. He asked my brother-in-law questions like what we were doing. My sister was studying accounting at a polytechnic college while I was studying engineering at the University of Nigeria. Universities are more superior to polytechnic according to Nigerians. University, especially University of Nigeria, was tough to get into and he did his undergraduate course at the University of Nigeria. I was studying engineering and girls who are doing these hard courses usually impress men. I think that proves the girl is smart or something. I think that made him proceed in my direction in the first place. He said from the pictures he thought my sister was finer.

Chidiebere: (looking at Ifeyinwa) I just want to let you know you happened to be the first person I called. I asked what she was doing to my friend (Ifeyinwa's brother-in-law). He said she was in her second year of engineering. I said what the heck, I don't want a second year student because engineering is a five-year program back in Nigeria. I did not want anyone younger than 23 years old because they are very immature. They have no idea about the world. I did not want to mess with someone who was clueless. I finally convinced myself and said let's give it a shot. I called her in Nigeria and we talked on the phone. We continued to talk on the phone for almost a year before I visited Nigeria to meet her. I was still talking to other girls while talking to her. I even met some other girls when I visited Nigeria

Ifeyinwa: (staring at Chidiebere) That I did not know about!

Chidiebere: (laughing) Why would you know about it? I met some other girls and her in Nigeria. I calculated how long it would take me to bring her to the US and decided it was worth moving forward with this relationship.

WHEN THE DEAL WAS SEALED:

Ifeyinwa: We have several traditional rituals that need to happen before we can get married. He has to come with his parents to my house to knock on the door.

Chidiebere: I had to knock on her door to tell her parents I am interested in their daughter.

Ifeyinwa: Traditionally, the parents are not supposed to know we know each other because parents did not support courtship traditionally. They come and tell the girl's parents indirectly, "I saw a ripe mango (or orange) in your family I want to pluck." If the parents have multiple girls, they line their daughters so the boy's family can choose the one. That was the traditional way. Now things have changed. Chidiebere's family came and told my father they were interested in me. My daddy said he had to consult his kindred's before accepting the proposal. In Igbo culture, one person does not own the child. The community owns the child. So my daddy talked to me and upon my acceptance, he talked to his kindred's and relations. They then decided on the date when they can come and pay the bride price. In Igbo culture, once the boy pays a bride price or dowry, you are engaged and the girl is no longer available. We paid the bride price and that's how we got engaged.

Chidiebere: I paid the bride price. We did not pay the bride price because it is the groom's responsibility to pay the price. It is very expensive to get married in Nigeria.

Ifeyinwa: We had a traditional wedding in Nigeria. As part of the rituals, we had to get a cow to feed the kindred's.

Chidiebere: They give you a list, which includes food, drinks, bicycle, etc. It differs from one town to the other. Some people are very greedy while some take it easy.

Ifeyinwa: It's not just the boy who has to pay for things. When they get married, there is something called the Iduno whereby the girl's parents have to buy gifts for the girl to take to her husband's house. Traditionally, they buy kitchen utensils for the girl to take to her husband's house because they believed the girl's place was in the kitchen. They also buy boxes of wrapper (traditional Nigerian attire). Once a girl was married, the clothes she wore were different than what the single girls wore. Single girls do not tie wrapper (traditional Nigerian attire), married women do. Married women do not wear skirts and pants. They tie wrapper. Things have changed now. The box of wrapper has changed into a car now.

Chidiebere: In conclusion, we had a traditional wedding in Nigeria, a court wedding in the United States, and we had a church wedding in Nigeria after a year of being here. Court wedding is for the government and official purposes. Kindred's only value the church wedding because they can eat and have fun.

Ifeyinwa in America

I came to America on February 14, 2003. I traveled alone on my first time in an airplane. I was not scared because I focused all my thoughts on meeting him. I took the long flight to America because I really wanted to meet him. I never knew what turbulence was and did not expect any. When the flight first moved, I thought we were going to fall down. The turbulence was scary, but what made the ride scarier was the silence around. I looked around several times to make sure I was traveling with other human beings and that they did not fall during the flight. When the flight attendant asked me for drinks, I could not understand anything she said. I stared at her wondering what language she was speaking in. I think about it today and I am sure she could not understand me either. I made a friend on the plane that helped me survive the long flight to my honey. We finally landed in San Francisco, California.

I saw Chidiebere standing at the airport and his face made the entire journey worthwhile.

I knew about America from watching TV and had high expectations of my life here. The way America was talked about on TV and in Nigeria made me believe roads were made of gold. I thought my life would include wearing high heels in my house and walking down the stairs from one room to the other room in my mansion. I was prepared for the glamorous American life. As soon as Chidiebere picked me up from the airport and we drove on the freeway, I was disappointed to see the roads were made of cement and not gold. I still had my hopes for the mansion. The hopes were crashed when he opened the door to our one bedroom apartment in Hayward, California. I had never lived in a one-bedroom apartment in my entire life. I give my husband a hard time to this day about my welcome here, and he faults the movies I watched. He bursts out laughing every time I tell him he cheated me of a big mansion.

I started at a junior college in 2003. Chidiebere was not messing around when he said he wanted a girl who was doing her own thing. Before I could move to America, my husband asked me to bring my transcripts from Nigeria so I could start at a junior college and then transfer to a university. I did not understand what a junior college was. Remember in Nigeria, polytechnic was different from university. I thought junior college was similar to that and told him I did not want to step down by attending junior college. He told me they offered the same general education courses as the university and I could transfer in two years. He wasn't going to pay international fees at the university when he could pay lesser fees at a junior college. He convinced me and I started at Chabot College. Junior college was not as hard as university in terms of culture shock. However, I could not understand the accent here. The language barrier was a big deal for me. I started taking a course on C++ programming. In spite of my difficulty with accents, I asked questions in classes. My professors often responded with a "huh" because they could not understand my accent. I was not shy and my personality played a big role in helping me adjust to the American ways. I met one of my friends in my class named Jose who helped me a lot. He had the patience to work with me on the lectures. I think we spent so much time together that he was able to understand my accent.

America is extremely accepting to one's uniqueness. When they couldn't understand my accent, they had the patience to hear me out again. They asked me where my accent was from sometimes, but never showed if they were angry or upset. My husband was the one who embarrassed me a lot because of my accent. Initially I couldn't understand other accents. For instance if I spoke to an Indian person with an Indian accent or a Spanish person with a Spanish accent, I could not understand them. Chidiebere always asked me, "Really, you cannot understand them!" I wanted to communicate with people, but could not understand them. Every time I had to communicate with a new person, I was scared. I did not tell Chidiebere about it. The first time he took me to his office, I was not very comfortable. I dreaded it for days leading to it. I was very scared, but did not tell him. I was scared because I could not understand them.

While accents scared me, computer skills challenged me. I remember I was in San Jose State and had to partner with this guy for an engineering lab project. We had to use the computer for the project. My lab partner was really fast. After trying to catch up with him for ten minutes or so, I told him I was not following him and asked if he could slow down. He mockingly looked at me and asked if I had not learned how to type and use a computer before in front of everyone. He was very rude. I told him we were supposed to do this project together. If he had problems with me, we could ask the professor to have us assigned to new lab partners. After giving him a piece of my mind, I held my composure long enough to reach the bathroom where I cried my eyes out.

During my initial years in Chabot College and San Jose State University, I met people who were willing to help me. They understood I was a foreigner and were patient with me. I also met people who weren't so nice to me. I did not know how to make friends and meet new people. I met people who eventually became my good friends and helped me socialize. I graduated from San Jose State with an electrical engineering degree.

Years have dawned since I came to America. The challenges have grown from accents to raising my two sons as Nigerians in America.

LIFE IN AMERICA

It is very important for both Chidiebere and I that our sons speak our native language. We wanted them to be rooted to Nigeria, so we gave them Nigerian names. Whenever their names are called, any Nigerian in the room will know they are from Nigeria. We wanted to ensure they retained their identity. My husband speaks in our native language to them more than I do. Sometimes it is easier to get them moving by speaking in English. Chidiebere speaks to them in our language. He believes their young brains can grasp new languages faster now than when they are older. We took them back to Nigeria for the first time in 2015 because we felt they were at the age where they could understand their cousins and their identity. We hope to take them back to Nigeria every two or three years. It is important they know where they come from. In America you are on your own. You barely know your neighbors. In Nigeria, everyone has your back no matter what. Everyone knows each other in Nigeria and is more family oriented. We would love for our sons to know and understand our language and culture. It is their identity. The United States of America and Nigeria are poles apart in culture, each good in its own way. As much as we like American culture, we do not want our children to have American culture. They are Nigerian and it is important to both of us that our children learn the Nigerian way of life and culture.

How I Changed in America

Ifeyinwa: I have changed the way I talk. I have learned to pronounce words differently. In Nigeria, when we went to college we wore heels and carried a purse. After coming here, I had to learn to dress down while going to college because in America people carry a backpack and wear sneakers. Nigerian men like women with hair, so we did not shave our legs there. I had to learn to shave my legs since coming here. College was hard because I did not have a good foundation from Nigeria in Math. Being an engineering student, I was expected to have a good foundation in Math. My husband helped me a lot and supported me. He gave me time to study, helped me with research, and tried to make my life easy in any way possible. I think computers were something I had to learn since I came here. My kids probably know the computer better than I do even now.

Visiting Nigeria

Ifeyinwa: I have imbibed several good things from American culture into my life. There are several things about Nigerian culture that I don't like. I find it hard to fit into some of the everyday situations in Nigeria. I think it is very visible to people there as well. Sometimes they say I have an attitude, or I don't behave well, or I have lost my manners and am being disrespectful because I cannot fit in. I am just being who I am. For instance, when I visited Nigeria in 2015, I was offered a drink when I was visiting someone. I received the drink with my left hand. We generally receive drinks with our right hand. It is considered rude to receive things with left hand. I did not realize at the time that I was using my left hand. One of the ladies had already corrected me once. She made a big deal about it, and what was a bigger deal was that I received the drink from a man with my left hand. Situations like that make me realize how much I have changed since living here. Little things that never bothered me my whole life, like the ceiling being low, bothers me there. My head was almost touching the ceiling. I speak English, which I think is different from how I speak here, but they always taunt me saying I speak American English.

Chidiebere: Even though I have lived here longer than her, I am adaptable. When I visit Nigeria, it's like I have always lived there and I fit in easily. She goes there and she is like I won't do this or go there. When we went back for our church wedding, she had lived here for a year at that point. She gave her siblings such a hard time about the details that I felt bad for them. She does not take public transportation. She wants to be driven everywhere or she wants to drive herself.

Ifeyinwa: In Nigeria, the back seat of the car has four or five people in a three person seat. They are packed like sardines. People you don't know are sitting with you. The weather is too hot and people are sweating. I don't want to be in the same car as them.

Chidiebere: She does not like public transportation. That's the underlying issue. Even if I were to rent a car for just us, she does not like public transportation.

Ifeyinwa: Each time I go to Nigeria, I see a different Nigeria from when I was growing up there. Western influences, such as Kim Kardashian, have slowly eroded the culture. People who have no idea about the west are mimicking the west. Traditions and cultures are slowly changing for the worse. People like us who live in the West understand the importance of maintaining our culture.

HOME

Ifeyinwa: (while Chidiebere shook his head in acceptance) I have lived in America since 2003. It has been over twelve years now. America has changed me and I have learned a lot having lived here for so many years. I have come to realize no matter what I do, home will always be home. Home is Nigeria. That is where I come from, that is who I am, and that defines me. I miss my family every second of the day. I have built a home here, I have kids here, but I also have a family back in Nigeria. The family I was born into and the family that is my identity. You see so many things going on here. There is discrimination everywhere. As a black woman in America, I have experienced discrimination more than once. It is almost omnipresent everywhere. Every time someone sees me, they see a black person. They see my accent. Even though we are welcome here, we have a boundary we cannot cross. We are reminded of that every day. I have begun to appreciate who I am and the importance of having an identity. My home and my identity will forever be Nigeria

You Will Be Slaughtered Alive!

I LAY AWAKE ON MY BED, battling the fears of a new beginning. Tomorrow was a new day and a new beginning. My family was moving to California, America. When I first found out we were immigrating to California, I was excited. I knew about America from the many movies and TV shows I had watched, both Bollywood and Hollywood. I told my friends about it, unable to conceal my excitement. As the days neared for my departure, my excitement was replaced by fear, nervousness, separation anxiety, and more fear. I watched dawn appear in the horizon and felt the excitement in the air. I watched the sunrise knowing it was going to be my last sunrise in the place I considered home. My mom, three sisters, and I loaded into my uncle's car as we made our way to Islamabad International Airport.

That was fifteen years ago, yet I vividly remember the day like it was yesterday. As we began our journey to the airport, I tried to memorize every detail of my life in Pakistan until then. I recalled the street corners where I hung out with my friends, the school yard that played ally to our games, the trees that provided shade on warm summer afternoons – I memorized every detail, hoping to store it for posterity. I watched the different landscapes as our car made its way to Islamabad airport. Before I could comprehend, the bold letters signaling the airport appeared in the horizon. I felt tears trickle down my cheeks as reality stared me in the eye.

I don't remember much of the commotion except following my mother around the airport after parking our car. Suddenly I was jolted to reality and found myself standing at the terminal, waiting to board the flight to the United States of America. I had called Pakistan my home for the past ten years of my life. I was heartbroken and did not want to leave my home. I looked at the family I was leaving behind and memorized every little detail about them. I feared I would never see them again and the thought made me cry. A glass door divided us. I wanted to break through it and go back home. I stood there fighting tears and watching my cousins 100 feet behind the glass door. Neither of us knew if we would ever see each other again.

At the check-in counter, a young Pakistani man of medium height and wearing a white uniform helped us with the formalities. He was one of the airport personnel crew who was supposed to check our documents and check-in our bags. He looked at my boarding pass and at me. He did this multiple times and with each time the perplexed look on his face kept growing. "Ma'am, is your final destination United States of America?" he asked me. I was still crying and responded with a nod. I could guess the source of his confusion by then. I should have looked happy going to the United States of America, the country every person dreams of living in. On the contrary, I was crying my eyes out like I was being sent to Antarctica or the North Pole. The young Pakistani man kept looking at me. Eventually, when my family moved away from me, he approached and asked me, "Can I help you escape these people you are with? I can help you. I know why you are crying. A young girl like you should not be married away. Let me help you. I can take you back to your family or wherever you want to go." I was stuck at the word married. I smiled for the first time in over twenty-four hours. He assumed I was a child bride on her way to meet her husband in the United States for the first time, accompanied by her mother-in-law and sisters-in-law. It felt strangely comforting to be a naïve child bride in my own fairy tale for a few hours.

After gathering myself back to reality, I explained why I was crying. I was not a helpless girl or a mail order bride. I was going to the United States of America, the land of dreams and opportunities, along with my mom and sisters. It ought to have been the happiest day of my life, or anyone's life, but it wasn't because I was leaving loved ones behind. Although I didn't acknowledge it, when he offered his help I desperately wanted him to rescue me from my current situation. I did not want to leave Pakistan and so badly wanted someone to help me stay here forever. I wanted someone to swing a magic wand and turn Pakistan into America. I wanted a genie to make the streets of Pakistan safe, ensure law and order was in place, and equal rights existed for men and women. I wanted someone to turn Pakistan into the immigrant dream America was, where Afghan immigrants like me could have opportunities like everyone else. If a genie could transform Pakistan into America, I would have no reason to leave. My life would be perfect, filled with love and surrounded by the people who made it home.

As I walked through the terminal into my flight, it felt too familiar. While most people would have been petrified to start a new life in a foreign country, I was an experienced person at sixteen. I had been there before and vividly remember the day when I bid adieu to the country my family had called home for generations. I was six years old when my family eloped from Kabul, Afghanistan, to Pakistan during the Russian invasion. I remembered wondering why we were fleeing home like it was yesterday. I had called Pakistan home since I was six years old. Pakistan was the only home I ever really knew. I grew into a young lady in Pakistan. I had to learn a new language while attending grade school and eventually assimilated into the culture as I cleared grades and finally graduated high school. Pakistan had begun to feel familiar and I was starting to feel at home when I was told we were immigrating to another strange foreign land. I would have to start over again, except this time language was not a barrier. I had attended the British school system in Pakistan and was fluent in English.

Our journey to America was long and tiring. We were provided with the cheapest flights with multiple stops and delays to San Francisco. As I sat on different flights going to places besides San Francisco, it felt like I was going to another planet. I checked my tickets multiple times confirming San Francisco was our last destination. I felt like ET trapped on a flight to a faraway planet, except in my situation it was home. By the time I landed in San Francisco, I was exhausted beyond words. Little did I know the adventure was just beginning. In between all the exhaustion, I was feeling the excitement of a new start and was looking forward to comparing San Francisco to the image I had formed in the months before our trip. The excitement soon turned to anxiety as my family and I lined up at the immigration line. I was confused and overwhelmed as we entered the room with the "residents" and visitors" line. We followed directions from the officers and followed the line. After an exhausting three-hour immigration grilling, we finally walked out of the airport and caught a glimpse of the city we were going to call home. We made our way to our hotel in a cab. As we drove through the streets of San Francisco, I was completely in awe of the beauty in front of me. San Francisco was exactly as I had imagined it to be, completely mesmerizing. San Francisco did not seem too bad and I remember thinking I could definitely get used to living there.

As our car made its way through San Francisco, I could see San Francisco airport behind us in bold letters. It felt surreal. The TV show Full House had been my guide to all things San Francisco. I thought I knew San Francisco from the many episodes of Full House engraved in my memory. It was beautiful on TV, but watching the San Francisco skyline in person was spectacular. The city was prettier than what I had seen on TV and it felt unreal. I couldn't believe I was actually in San Francisco. I felt the doubts melt away and felt assured my life in America was going to be incredible to say the least.

I had my American lifestyle all figured out. When I was told we were going to America, I was not sure about how my life would change, but I was certain I would be living in one of those high-rise skyscrapers. I had seen it on TV, and thought it was the American way of living. Everyone in America lived in tall buildings and during my initial drive through San Francisco I was even more certain of it. I watched my car drive past one tall building after another. With each passing building I thought maybe the next one would be my home. Before long, our car had driven past San Francisco. I was confused as our car moved past the pretty sights of San Francisco into the deep streets of East Oakland.

East Oakland was nothing like San Francisco. There were no tall buildings and bridges. The buildings around us were old, making the streets of Pakistan appear more beautiful than I remembered. We met with the agency responsible for our American move. They showed us our apartment and explained this was the best they could do for newly arrived Afghan refugees like us. Our apartment was on the second floor of a two floor building, deep in the ghettos of Oakland. I walked out on the porch and stared at reality ahead of me. I did not know the word ghetto until much later. Initially whenever I heard the word, I thought it was a word for our neighborhood. I was living in the American ghettos and it felt cool. We never had a word to describe my Pakistan neighborhood. Eventually I realized it was not a positive word. I came to America to live in skyscrapers and now I was walking the ghettos.

I had never heard of Oakland before our car made its way into East Oakland. I was completely oblivious to Oakland's reputation in crime and homicide. My survival in Oakland for the first three years of my American life was a true testament to the saying ignorance is bliss. Each day I walked the streets of Oakland with a big smile on my face. I was completely unaware of the crimes in our block. I accepted every form of greeting or compliment with a big smile and thank you. It never crossed my mind that some of these people I was talking to could be affiliated to a gang or could potentially be carrying weapons and guns. It did not matter because the America I had envisioned did not have crimes. I had made the journey around the world and beyond to reach America, the America portrayed as a dreamland where everything good happened. The America where dreams come true, and immigrants and refugees like me formed the crust of the land. The America I had watched on TV and envisioned did not have crimes. Why would I leave the comforts of Pakistan to forge a life in America if there were crimes? Oh no, America was definitely not like Pakistan and crimes did not exist, or so I believed.

We were not the first Afghan refugees to make America our home. Our agency had helped several people like us. As we were figuring out America, we were introduced to several other Afghans like us. We felt at ease in the company of these people who had been through some of what we had. We often visited each other like we did back home in Afghanistan. Whenever we invited them over to our house, they were very reluctant to visit us. They made excuses, and in some instances invited my family back to their place. It always confused me why they were reluctant to visit us. We wondered if we were doing something wrong when they came over. It took us over three years before we realized it wasn't us, but Oakland that was the problem. We finally bid adieu to Oakland after three years in the ghettos. As soon as we moved to Fremont, the Afghan community was more open to visiting us. The grunts stopped and so did the excuses. I realized people were healthier after we had moved to Fremont, away from the ghettos of Oakland. They no longer had headaches and the flu on the day we invited them over for dinner or tea.

The three years in Oakland was an eye opener to an American virgin like me. I realized income levels divided the communities. Rich people lived in nicer and more secure areas of the city and the poor ones were cramped up in low-income areas. As we walked through the streets of Oakland, we were made aware of this divide every day. The Oakland hills, with its big mansions, stared us in the eye while we walked the streets of East Oakland living our lives. The divide was evident everywhere we went. The American dream we came here for seemed further away than ever. It seemed much closer when I walked into the Pakistan airport. Although we warmed up to East Oakland, I knew I wanted to be in the spaciousness of Oakland's hills. Well not exactly Oakland's hills, but away from the low-income areas of America. I left family and friends in Pakistan for a more secure life in America. The ambience of my surrounding did not bother me, but the lack of security was the primary reason we decided to move to America. I realized to live my American dream of a safe and secure environment, I would have to work hard to afford one of those tall buildings. I left behind family and friends to live my American dream and I was going to achieve it no matter what.

Although the American dream seemed far-fetched sitting in my East Oakland apartment, I devised a plan to achieve it. I knew at 16 years of age, I would have to attend college and get a decent paying job to afford the tall buildings. I would need to sustain my career to continue living in those buildings. America was the land of opportunities and I was going to make the most of my life here. I did my research on the next logical step for me. I already received my high school diploma, so the next step was community college. I walked into community college brimming with positivity. I had very good high school grades and believed I was an asset to the college. My positivity started taking a dive when I saw the lady at the college stare at my transcripts with a perplexed look. I tried to stay positive through it all, until I was rejected based on my age. At 16 years of age, I was too young for college. Even if she were to admit me at 16, my high school diploma did not state the grade I had completed.

I was crushed and felt tears flowing down my cheeks as I stood there listening to her. It felt like my life was over before beginning. I starved myself for two days. I was on the verge of passing out from exhaustion when I decided I was going to attend college no matter what. If American high school was my gateway to university, then that's what I was going to do. I pulled myself together, gathered all pieces of my shattered dream, and visited a high school for admission.

I could not sleep all night and woke up before my alarm went off. I was nervous, excited, and ready to begin my American journey. It was my first day at high school. I did everything to make a good first impression. Back home I was my teacher's favorite student and I wanted to make sure I established that in America as well. I packed my bag, dressed up, and was on my way to high school.

As I walked the hallways of my high school, I saw students everywhere relaxing and laughing with each other. I could feel eyes follow me. I looked up and was completely mortified at what I saw. It felt like a fashion show with girls dressed in the latest fashions with makeup-clad faces lined up along the hallways. All my life I wore uniforms to school and I expected that walking into school until reality stared at me. My confidence was still high as I walked the hallways to the principal's office. As I walked, I glanced at myself in one of the windows. I wasn't aware of my lack of fashion sense until I walked into high school. I was dressed in high-rise jeans, t-shirt and sneakers. My hair was in a ponytail. My confidence hit an all-time low, as I stood there wondering how I was going to survive. "You are going to be slaughtered and eaten alive," a voice echoed in my head. The looks I got in the hallways made me wonder who among these people would want to befriend a girl in high-rise jeans and barely combed hair.

I found out later I had walked in during recess. I was used to the British school system where we had set schedule for the entire school.

We might have different classes in each period, but the time for recess was the same. It was very rare to see relaxed students in high school and this surprised me. "You are going to be slaughtered and eaten alive," the voice echoed again as I made my way to the Principal's office. The principal welcomed me into her office and looked at my high school diploma. "You will have to complete 11th and 12th grade here," she told me. I nodded in acceptance as the voice echoed again. She helped me pick my classes and gave me all the information I would need to be successful in high school. She was nice to me, but it did not matter. I knew I would not survive high school looking the way I did. I felt like ET again walking the hallways of school. People looked at me like I was a goofball. No one smiled at me. I walked out of the principal's office promising to start school the next day, but I knew I had only one option ahead of me - I had to do whatever it took to get an admission in the community college.

I could not wait for dawn, as I lay in bed nervous and scared. My American dream was in jeopardy if I could not get admission at the community college. I went back to the community college and met the same counselor who denied my admission. I cried in front of her, begging her to admit me. I challenged her I would pass every test she required of me, if only she gave me a chance. She looked at me for few minutes and contemplated her moves as I stood there with tears in my eyes. She obliged and told me I would have to take the test right then. The assessment test included trigonometry and college level English. A few hours later, she walked out of her office with a startled look on her face. I was nervous, but seeing her expression made me all the more scared. She handed me my scores and broke out into a big smile. She told me she was honored to have me at her college. I was stoked and could not control my tears of joy. I knew then I had passed the biggest test of my life yet. She did not expect a kid from a third world country with an unverified paper that said high school diploma to pass with such high grades. I had always been a nerd, but standing there holding the key to my American dream made being a nerd even sweeter.

If nerds had a club, I could have been the president of that club. I was a nerd all my life. I still believe I am and, like most nerds, fashion was never important to me. I never wore big glasses like the stereotype, but I did wear jeans, t-shirts, low ponytails and sneakers for as long as I can remember. Fashion was never important until I walked into high school on that dreadful day when I felt like Ugly Betty. I was terrified of college and believed it was going to be worse than high school. After all, the students there were all adults. On the contrary, everyone in the office was super nice. Before I could start college, I did my research on how I could make my college affordable for my mother. I applied for financial aid to help with non-resident tuition and was thrilled to pay for college myself. I was grown up, or at least I felt grown up at sixteen. I picked my classes and scratched each day in the calendar waiting for D-Day restlessly.

I woke up earlier than I was required to for my first day of college. I walked into college nervous, but the day ended with excitement and surprises. Everyone was nice and helped me through my first day. I realized soon I was one of the youngest in my classes. I was pretty much non-existent in my classes until midterms and quizzes happened. Suddenly I was thrust to the forefront and nicknamed "little smarty-pants" by my classmates. I could never figure out if the nickname was because of my scores or my very exotic name. I had been an Afghan living in Pakistan for most of my life, but everyone seemed to easily pronounce my name. While other Arabic names posed an issue, my Afghan name was a cakewalk for everyone. Everything changed when I stepped foot in America. I went from Shaima to Shameeya, Shayna, Shamaya, and Shymaya instantly and it continues to this day.

I continue to ponder on why Starbucks needs a name while ordering coffee. I decided to go to Starbucks to get a cup of coffee after being here for a while. I had by then heard several bad versions of my name and had even thought about officially changing my name to something else. I ordered my coffee and was about to pay for it when the girl asked me for my name. I told her Shaima. She looked perplexed and asked if I could repeat my name again. I said Sally, giving birth to my alter self. In restaurants when they ask for my name, I call myself Sara. Sara and Sally are the American alter egos of the ethnic Shaima, but unlike Shaima they are always pronounced correctly and never stared at with a baffling look.

America was the land of opportunities to immigrants like me. We always stood on the other side imagining an America full of opportunities with tall buildings and educated people. I always thought everyone in America had a four-year degree and was highly educated. It seemed like the most logical explanation for all the inventions. When I came here I was amazed at how many people did not avail the opportunities available. In college, I was surprised to see people in their late thirties, forties, and even sixties attending classes with me. In my country, college was right after high school. If one decided to skip college, they missed their chance. It was refreshing to know America provided a second chance at education with no concrete age limit.

It took me two years at a community college and three years at San Jose State University to finally receive my electrical engineering degree. Before I knew it, I was graduating from college having achieved step one of my American dream. It was an emotional day for my family and me. As I walked to receive my degree, I saw my family in tears. The pride in my mother's eyes let me know it was not just my dream, but also theirs. I was continuing the legacy of my father, who was an electrical engineer as well. I was beyond proud of my accomplishments.

After fifteen years in America, an engineering degree, six years of work experience, and a marriage, I have completely assimilated to the ways of this country. I came here as a refugee fleeing a country I called home and tried to make America, or precisely California, my home. I have accepted America as my home, but I am not sure if America has accepted me as her own. I have an American citizenship. As a true citizen, I continue to abide by the rules, pay taxes when due, and even go to my jury duty calls. Yet, every time I walk on the street with my traditional clothing or my headscarf, I get stared at as an outsider. I am reminded each time of being a refugee, except now I am an American passport-holding refugee. After fifteen years of calling America my home, I have realized no matter how much I assimilate with America, I will always be an Afghan American. The country I called home for the first six years of my life will always be my identity. Qabeli, Palaw, and Bolani (Afghan dishes) will continue to tug my heartstrings over a burger and fries. I will forever belong to Afghanistan, no matter where I live.

It Is So Colorful...Can I Touch?

I DRAGGED MY TIRED BODY out of the flight and through the tunnel. I felt frail and exhausted after the long journey to Denver, Colorado. I reached the end of the tunnel and stood there stumped. "Welcome to America Liti and Bobby," read the banners on strangers. Colorful balloons, flowers, gifts, and eager faces waited to welcome us. The commotion and chaos bothered me; the strange faces exhausted my already tired body. I was far from trying to pretend happiness in the wake of strangers. I barely smiled to acknowledge the twenty people who came to welcome me to the strange land I had decided to traverse in the name of love. I did not care to introduce myself or ask them about themselves. I did not care because I never wanted to make this journey. I wanted to be left alone and all I really cared for was a bed. The year was 1998. I had followed the love of my life to Denver, Colorado. I had been married for nine days before I decided to pack my belongings to follow the man I had known since I was a child. I remember that day and the days leading to it like it was yesterday.

My husband and I grew up together our entire lives. We met as children in Orissa (now called Odisha), a state in the east of India. The state was known for its beautiful sculptures, monuments, temples, wildlife, and beaches. I spent my growing years moving with my family wherever my dad's government job took us. Yet, I had the most sheltered childhood amidst the right balance of city and scenic landscape. I never imagined leaving India to make a home in America until 1991, when my then boyfriend told me he was moving to America. We spent hours speaking on the phone in the seven years we were apart. In those moments he told me about his life in America. He ate home cooked meals, went to college, and often pictured a life similar to the one I was living in India. He portrayed an America where the roads were wider, cleaner, and houses had no fences. It's America with no stray dogs, where the grass is always green; flowers were never plucked so fences were not required. When we spoke about marriage, he proposed the idea of us living in America. I shrugged it off. I believed I could make him settle in India with me. I tried relentlessly to persuade him to move back to India. He did not budge. In 1998, after seven years of long distance phone calls, I followed my love to the United States of America. A couple days before our marriage, I stood in line at the US consulate for my visa to America. Nine days after our marriage I was on a flight to Denver with my new husband.

The unexpected chaos at the airport exhausted me. After ignoring all the people who had come to welcome us at the airport, we made our way to our apartment. My husband's friends had cleaned and decorated the apartment with flowers. I walked into the apartment as everyone looked at me hoping to see the excitement on my face over the surprise they had in store for me. They were hoping for me to jump with joy as I walked on the rose petals they had spread all over. I took the first breath of air, looked at my husband, and asked him, "What is that smell?" They had placed air freshener plugins all around the apartment. The smell bothered me. For the next few minutes, everyone ran around the house trying to discard all the air freshener plugins. My first day in America was turning out to be a disaster, but I had high hopes for the next day after I slept. I woke up the next morning feeling just as groggy. I threw up for the next few days. I did not have any medical insurance, but I was so sick my husband decided to take me to the hospital. I was diagnosed with altitude sickness. Denver, being a high altitude city, played spoil-sport to my American homecoming.

The altitude sickness was a small thorn in my happily ever after. I was ready for my American bliss with my new husband. I decided to be the good Indian wife by cooking some food for him. I opened the refrigerator looking for ingredients and chanced upon some tube look-ing things. I had no idea what they were. I found out later that day they were called sausages. I was disgusted by how they looked and made him throw them out. I had never cooked a meal when I was growing up in India. I was the youngest in my family. I might have stirred some dishes, but never cooked anything from scratch. My husband believed I could make tea and omelet. I wanted to dispel that myth. I decided to make some Indian sautéed potatoes. As the oil started getting hot, I put the cut potatoes and onions in the oil. While I was sautéing the dish, I start-ed feeling sick to my stomach. I had no clue what bothered me, but for a potato addict like me it broke my heart. I took pride in eating potatoes for breakfast, lunch, and dinner. I tried various combinations of pota-toes (Russell, white), onions (yellow, white), and oil for the next month before I found a winning combination that worked. I called my mother every day from America for recipes. She guided me through every step of the recipe. I insisted on having her on the phone until the dish was fully cooked and the oven was turned off. The phone bills used to be $600-$700 each month while I got my cooking lessons. I was so im-pressed with my newly acquired cooking skills I started a website where I posted my recipes. I had mastered an Indian lentil curry and a potato dish that became staple dish at all my parties for years to come.

In between my battles in the kitchen, I had to go shopping for clothes. As soon as I landed in Denver, I knew my tropical Indian clothing would freeze me to death. I wanted to go shopping with my husband, but he insisted I go with some of his friends. He believed the girls could help pick better clothes than he could. India in the 90's did not have big shopping malls, chain stores, or designer labels. Shopping has always been a chore I barely enjoyed. I was not thrilled to go shopping with strangers I could not understand. They picked me up from my house. As we were driving, one of the girls excitedly said, "Let's begin at Gap." I was confused as to what Gap was. The only gap I knew did not involve shopping in any way or form. As I sat there perplexed, they said we were going to the mall and if we could not find what we were looking for we would go to another mall. They told me the malls we were visiting. It did not matter because I had no idea what it meant. They could have said we were going to Walmart for all I cared. It would have been bigger than any store I had ever been in. At the mall they threw out names, like Levi's Silvertab or 501, while I stood there confused. We walked into Gap. I walked around and picked a few t-shirts and jeans when the girls told me I should try the clothes in the fitting room. I had no idea what a fitting room was. I tried four outfits before I started getting annoyed. I wasn't used to the concept of trying clothes out before buying, and moreover doing it for fun. It was not fun for me. It had been two hours too long and we hadn't bought anything yet. They decided on going to a different mall. I had reached my breaking point by then. "I want to go home," I told them. They looked at me surprised. "We just started shopping," one of the girls told me. I forced them to take me home. I could wear my salwar kameez (Indian attire) from India that took 15 minutes to buy for the rest of my life if need be. In India we bought the cloth for the tailor to stitch. I thought that was complicated, but standing at the Levi's fitting room trying on different jeans made me realize how easy life had been in India.

Denver has a big food festival during Labor Day weekend each year. I had been in America for a month when my husband decided to give me the American food festival experience. I was excited. I took pride in being very open to different kinds of food. Unlike other Indians, I ate chicken, goat, shrimp, and fish. I was more equipped to deal with American food than the vegetarians. We just walked into the festival when I asked my husband, "What is that meat burning smell?" I was sure someone had burned food and messed up big time. My husband explained American open pit BBQ to me. Burned meat did not sound appetizing to me. The American food festival was not my cup of tea. My husband loves Chinese food and can eat it for lunch, breakfast, and dinner. I have enjoyed Chinese food in India, but when I first went to an authentic Chinese restaurant like Dim Sum, I couldn't take the smell. I have accompanied my husband and ordered Coke in Chinese restaurants. Even Coke bothered me. The smell in oriental stores bothered me. It took months before I could enjoy Chinese food in America.

When my husband told me we were going to settle in America, I was nervous about adapting here, living with my husband for the first time, and staying away from my family. Although I had several doubts, I was confident in my conversation skills. I had complete confidence in my English skills until I walked into Walmart or CVS in Denver to pick up some photographs. This was before the digital camera era when photo rolls were still being developed. I walked up to the counter confidently and told her, "I am here to pick up my pho-to-graphs". She stared at me and asked me to repeat. I checked to ensure it actually said photo pick-up area. I said, "I am here for my pho-to-graphs." She had no clue what I was saying. After repeating four more times, she finally heaved a sigh of relief while saying "photographs." While she was relieved, I was irritated and annoyed, wondering the difference between what she said and what I said. To this day, I have no idea why she couldn't understand my photographs.

When I first moved to America, I decided I was going to be the flag bearer to my culture. I wore my Indian attire at every opportunity possible. A few months into my stay in Denver, I wore my salwar kurta (Indian attire) while walking to the parking lot of our apartment. As I walked, I heard someone run after me. I saw this Caucasian lady gasping and running towards me. I thought maybe something was wrong as I checked for my keys and wallet. She stopped near me, gasping, and exclaimed, "Wow, your outfit is so beautiful. It is so colorful. I saw it through my window and had to come close to see it." I felt like an exotic animal at that point, but it got even better. "What is this called?" she asked me. I told her what it was called. After she regained her composure, she asked me, "Can I touch it?" I smiled back at her wondering if she actually asked to touch my clothes. I thought I misunderstood her because of her accent. After few minutes, she asked me again if she could touch it. I obliged, but in those moments I knew exactly what animals felt like when someone touched their fur. Denver in the late 90's did not have too many Indians or an active Indian community. Every time I wore my traditional attire, I got stared at.

In between all my food and shopping adventures, I missed my family back in India. I had been in America for five months when I decided to visit India. I came here on a fiancée visa. According to the visa, we had to be married within 30 days of my arrival in America. We got married as soon as I got here, so I knew I was legal here, but I wasn't sure what documentation I would need to go back home. I called the INS to enquire about the paperwork. The lady on the phone put me on hold while she located my file. I was excited knowing I was going back home. She came back on the line and told me, "We don't have your file." I could not understand American accents, but I was pretty sure I knew what she meant. I told her the specifics of when we sent the documents, but she confirmed she did not have any such file. My husband's lawyer had moved from Georgia around the time we sent him our documents. He never received my documents and I was officially an illegal immigrant in America. I was frustrated, scared, and nervous about our future. My husband decided to contact a famous lawyer who was referred to us by friends. He charged $275 for a phone consultation. After speaking to us he signed off saying a line that broke my heart: "No matter what you do, do not leave the country." My dreams to go back home were crumbled in a second. I was depressed, lonely, homesick, and sad. I moped around for close to a month. My husband watched me retreat into a shell. I woke up one morning after a month of moping and decided I was not going to be illegal in this country. I researched everything from fiancée visas to immigration parole documents for the next 15-20 days. After twenty days of relentless research, my husband and I walked into the INS office on a cold Denver morning at 3am. We waited until 10am, when we were finally called to the window. Instantly, the lady denied my paperwork, stating you should apply for change of status within 180 days of being in the United States. I was prepared for this moment. I asked her to show me where it says you need to apply within that duration. She checked on her computer and her face turned perplexed. She closed her window, walked inside, and talked to her peers. They then showed our case to her managers. Eventually, her manager came in and said, "You are right. It does not state you need to apply for change of status within 180 days of being here. You need to get married within 30 days of being in the country, which you did. You are approved!" I could not believe my ears. I got my status change, packed my bags, and went back home to India. It was a year and three months after I had arrived in America.

While my husband told me about the streets of America and houses with no fences, he did not introduce me to the most important aspect of American life: you have to do everything on your own. I was used to having maids and chauffeurs to help with daily chores. I had to learn to take care of my own chores. I felt like a caged bird for the first year and half in America. I did not have a work permit to work. I did not have a driver's license to drive. I could not figure out something as simple as getting from point A to point B. In India we called for an auto rickshaw, but here it looked like everyone could drive a car. I did not have friends to hang out with, and even if I did I was never one to spend hours in a friend's home. Each day I spent alone in my apartment, I got more depressed. Everything on television was alien to me. The news bored me after few hours, while the soap operas made me depressed. TV shows were not my cup of tea. The longer I stayed inside, the more depressed I started getting. I forced myself to go for walks during the day. My husband ensured we had errands each day so we could go out. He kept all shopping for weekdays so he could take me out for few hours. I did not miss the air outside. I missed going to work and being busy. I had always been busy in India. I worked until three days before my marriage as a manager for a financial institution in India.

After year and half of being here, I finally received my green card. I was excited to start working finally. I started on my job search as soon as I held my green card in my hand. I looked for financial job openings. Everything required certifications I did not have. My job description in India meant nothing here. I could go back to school for the certifications, but I did not want to study. I did not know what to do. I felt aimless for the first time in my entire life. My husband and I were strolling through the mall one day when we saw a posting for help at Dillard's. It was a part time position. My husband insisted I apply for it. I stared at him with my I-cannot-believe-you-want-me-to-work-as-a-sales-assistant look. I could not believe he would even suggest it. He convinced me to take the sales job in the interim while I found something permanent. I was learning how to drive a car and was not comfortable driving too far. This job was close to my home where I could either walk or drive. I was offended, but desperate for a job. I applied and a day later I was working as a sales assistant at Dillard's. Although I continued working at Dillard's, with each passing day I got more depressed. I did not know what I was doing with my life. I had gone from being a manager to a sales assistant at a store. I worked there for 15-20 days. During that stretch one of my co-workers told me about how she applied at a bank and got accepted to work there. With her guidance, I applied to a bank. A month and half later I started working at the bank as a teller.

While working at the bank made me feel better in comparison to the sales job at Dillard's, I had several instances where I pondered what I was doing with my life. I was working as a manager running a financial institution in India and now I was working as a teller at a bank. I fluctuated between being happy and depressed on most days. I found working as a teller challenging. I was still getting accustomed to the American ways. I continued having trouble understanding American English and accents. Simple things like greeting customers with a, "Hi, How are you?" was new to me. I had to force myself to incorporate some of these customary behaviors. While walking on the street, if someone asked me how I was, I wondered how it mattered to him or her. Initially I wanted it to stop, but with time I began adjusting to the American ways. It took me a few years, but I started feeling comfortable here. I made friends and was happy living here. Life started moving on slowly.

After years in Denver, we moved to California. California was unlike Denver in many ways. The weather was beautiful all year round. California had a big Indian population. I was no longer an exotic animal people wanted to touch. People walked around in saris and no one blinked an eye. I made friends in California and years sped by us. Before we realized, my husband and I had two sons. Before I could have my kids, I was idealistic in my approach. The girl who swore to wear Indian attire at every possible opportunity swore to ensure her son would speak Oriya (our language), eat Indian food, and be as Indian as possible. When my oldest son was younger, I spoke to him in our language in spite of my husband speaking predominantly in English at home. I was thrilled every time I heard him speak in our language. I knew I was doing something right. When my son was in kindergarten, I watched him converse with his friends. I noticed he was having trouble switching between the two languages. I could not stand to watch the dilemma he was facing. I decided if he was more comfortable conversing in English, then I would adjust to it. I learned to be flexible with my children just as I learned to be a mother. My children are four years apart. The older one was conversing primarily in English when the younger one was a baby. I can still bribe my older one to converse in Oriya sometimes, but my younger one finds it funny. However, my older one has an English accent while conversing in Oriya, but my younger has no accent when he repeats words after me.

It has been challenging raising children while holding a full time job. Initially I enforced going to temples and celebrating Diwali and other festivals. As the years progressed and life happened, everything fell through. My children did not eat Indian food when they were younger, but have taken a liking to Indian food with time and age. Initially when we visited India, we packed macaroni and other American foods for them. When we visited India in 2014, I did not use any of the food I had packed. They ate Indian food at home and occasionally we took them to KFC or Pizza Hut when they craved a change. I take solace knowing with time my children will become more Indian. I feel hope seeing my nephew, who was as American as you could find, embrace Indian culture and food as he started attending college. Now he goes to the temple every week, eats Indian food, and is an active member in the Indian association at his college. I watch my children growing up here and I am happy about the way I have raised them. They enjoy India almost as much I do. I have been taking them to India throughout the course of their young life. Yet, every time I go back home I feel a sense of regret when I watch my parents with them. They watch my kids as they converse. They cannot converse or understand them. I wish my children could speak Oriya so my parents can converse with them. I wish my parents would visit me sometimes. I have tried inviting them to America for a few months, but my parents, especially my father, would not visit us for even a month. I wish I could take my parents around and show them the world I have built here.

When I think in retrospect on the life I have lived in America, there are several things I am very proud about. I am proud about the life I have built. I have a beautiful home, my two children, and the life I live each day, be it work or home. I am in a happy space now, but I also remember the young girl who followed love to this land. I remember the moments of depression when I couldn't figure out the accent or get the job I dreamed about. It has been a journey filled with moments of pain, trials, and ultimately tribulation. America has also thrown some surprises along the way. I was shocked when I found out I would have to do everything from cleaning and cooking to driving by myself. I remember the first time I went back to India after over a year of being here. I got out of Calcutta airport and wondered why the air was so polluted with dust. My body had forgotten the smells I had grown up with each day. Yet, I had longed to go back home for so long I felt a sense of being home I had taken for granted. Since that trip I have made several trips to India. Each time I go back I still get the sense of being home, yet home has changed in some ways for me. America is where my home is, I have raised my kids here and my life is here. America has become my homeland, but India will always be my motherland. I was born in India, I have spent some of the most wonderful years of my life as a child in India, and my parents still live there. India is home and so is America. The emotions associated with India and America are different, but I feel at home in both places. When I am in America, I yearn to go back to India and spend time with my family. When I visit India for an extended period of time, I miss the warmth of my home in America. The memories are different, the ambience is contrasting, but my heart belongs to both India and America!

There are Some People Who are Coming to Take Me Away!

"WE NEED TO MOVE QUICKLY. There is no time to pack anything. Naseer, your uncle is waiting for you outside. He will take you to Ghazni," Agha Jan told us in Pashto. I looked into his eyes fearing the worst. I knew his answer before asking him, yet I did, "Agha Jan, are you coming to Ghazni with us?" The words that followed startled me more than the gunshots outside our house. He held me close while explaining why he wasn't going with us. My uncle was going to take us to our ancestral province Ghazni and Agha Jan would meet us there. We would then cross the border of Afghanistan to Pakistan through Ghazni. "There are some people who are coming to take me away," Agha Jan said, justifying his actions. My mother, siblings, and I accompanied my uncle to Ghazni as my father stayed behind, watching us leave. I turned several times to catch a glimpse of my Agha Jan. With each step I took, the blurrier his image became. I was scared for him and for us.

At nine years of age, I felt my life crumbling before my eyes. My family planned to flee the only country I had ever known. My uncle told us we were going to walk until we found a safe place to hitch a car ride to Ghazni from Kabul. My mother, siblings, and I walked from Kabul. I remember terrains changing, but the chaos of the missiles and rockets reminded us we were not safe yet. Each step seemed scarier than the previous one. As we walked, I remember wondering how the positivity I had sensed in Afghanistan not too long ago had turned into such mad-ness. As a nine year old, I felt anger at several things, the only place I had called home was now in a barrage of rockets and missiles, gunshots replaced the calmness in the air, and people were taking my Agha Jan away. As we walked our way to Ghazni, I wondered why my Agha Jan, a singer, would be taken away by people. I remember hearing the Russians were leaving Afghanistan and the Mujahedeen were taking over Kabul. For the first time in my young life, I had sensed positivity and excitement among my people.

For as long as I can remember, Afghanistan has always been war struck and invaded. Yet, the Afghanistan in the many stories my parents told us was different. I am yet to witness that Afghanistan. I was born during the Russian invasion of Afghanistan. I was the oldest son to my parents and second oldest to my sister. In spite of only knowing Afghanistan through the lens of war, I had the fondest memories of my country. I was born in Afghanistan, the streets bore witness to my childhood years, and the house we lived in was my security blanket through it all. I felt a sense of belonging in Afghanistan as I heard everyone around speak my language. I felt immense pride knowing my ancestors walked the land I was walking on. While it might seem weird for a nine year old to think of his war-ridden country with so much pride, I believe Afghan pride was in my blood. My father, Agha Jan, was a famous patriotic singer in Afghanistan. His music was very popular among Afghans. I could sense his music in the air of Afghanistan. I believe my love for Afghanistan began long before I really knew myself. As a child, I would listen to him recite poems about the greatness of the land we belonged to. He told me stories about our heroes and legends that fought for the dignity of Afghans. Those moments portrayed an Afghanistan different from the one I was living. The Afghan people were strong and brave people who fought for their country. I fell in love with the Afghanistan before the wars, missiles, and rockets. Through my Agha Jan's poetry, music, and words, I witnessed the Afghanistan my forefathers fought hard for.

In spite of growing up in an Afghanistan invaded by Russia, I don't ever remember wanting to leave my country. When I heard everyone talk about Russians leaving Afghanistan, I felt a sense of positivity in my surroundings. We were finally free and our own people could assume power. The Mujahedeen were expected to rebuild Afghanistan for the better. Afghanistan echoed the sounds of freedom as everyone rejoiced at being free. Instead, the same Mujahedeen groups who claimed to have sacrificed their lives to fight against Russia for Afghans were fighting amidst each other for power over Kabul. It did not take long before seven Mujahedeen groups started firing rockets and missiles at one another. I stood watching Kabul turn into a battlefield in the hands of the seven Mujahedeen groups. They did not care about the innocent civilians caught in the midst of this turmoil. The part of Kabul I called home came under heavy fire, being one of the strategic locations to attaining power over Kabul. It became very clear they did not care about anything but power. Things got ugly quickly. People started fleeing Kabul or moving to areas of lesser scrutiny. I watched all my neighbors flee Kabul for safer grounds. I never thought we would be fleeing Kabul, too, until my dad told me, "Naseer, your uncle is waiting for you outside."

After hours of walking by foot and traveling by car, we finally arrived at Ghazni. I was glad my mother and siblings were safe. I felt a sense of responsibility being the oldest son. Although we were all safe for now, my Agha Jan was not with us. "They are coming to take me," echoed in my head. We stayed in Ghazni with my uncle and his family for a month while waiting for my father. Each day we wondered how my Agha Jan was doing. After almost thirty days of shattered hope, we finally saw my dad for the first time since the day we walked to Ghazni. My family was in tears to be finally reunited again. As much as we wanted to enjoy the moment, it was time for us to leave our village in Ghazni. We couldn't stay in the village any longer, as the news of our location had reached the local Mujahedeen. Agha Jan echoed the words I had hated for a month: "The people will come get me if we don't leave now." He could see the confusion on our faces, wondering why the Mujahedeen wanted my Agha Jan. While my Agha Jan was not a political figure, his songs spoke against the Mujahedeen. The Mujahedeen, especially the ones who used religion to control people and spread hatred, feared my father's music. My father sang about patriotism. They feared his music had the power to gain the support of the Afghans to revolt against them. They saw my father as a threat. I remember thinking this was more serious than I expected it to be.

My father told us we were going to Quetta, Pakistan. I was overwhelmed with emotions as we crossed the border of Afghanistan into Pakistan. I could hear the rockets and missiles in the horizon. I should have felt relieved that my family and I were safe. I was happy to be safe, but I did not want to leave Afghanistan. I was deeply in love with my country. The songs and stories I heard reverberated in my head as we reached Quetta, Pakistan. Quetta was closest to Afghanistan. We stayed there for a year during which my father couldn't continue singing because the Mujahedeen could reach Quetta easily. We brought very little money with us from Afghanistan. Things got really hard for my family of eight. I could see the stress in my father's eyes as he wondered how he would feed six children and his wife without any income. My father had fans in Pakistan who helped make our ends meet. But eventually the Mujahedeen located us in Quetta and we were on the move again. We relocated each time Mujahedeen found us. We could not go outside to play with other children. My parents locked us in the house in fear of being caught by the Mujahedeen. While it was hard to acclimate ourselves in a foreign country, it became even harder when we couldn't socialize and make friends. Life kept getting worse as we struggled to survive in Pakistan. Streets no longer felt familiar and the sense of being home evaded us. After a year of relocating and moving around Quetta, we finally moved to Karachi in Pakistan.

Karachi was one of the bigger cities in Pakistan. It offered more security, being farther away from Afghanistan. We were allowed to socialize with others for the first time in a year. However, we realized everything was very expensive in Karachi. My father could not sing since the Mujahedeen were still in striking distance. Our finances depleted without any steady income. My younger brother and I decided to shoulder the responsibility to provide for our family. I was ten years old when I started working. We were too young to get a job, so we started selling boiled potatoes and eggs at grade schools in our area. We could not afford to send any of the kids to school, so my father home schooled us. We started getting educated on basic writing and reading skills in Farsi and Pashto. Our Pakistani neighbor, who was a teacher, offered to teach us Urdu, English, and other subjects such as math and science for free.

Although I was getting the required education, there was always emptiness in my heart. The emptiness grew each time I went to sell eggs and potatoes at grade schools during lunchtime. Children wearing uniforms surrounded me, but unlike me they were in school. I would often watch them play with each other during lunch. They did not have to sell snacks like me. I so badly wanted to be one of them. I would daydream about the day I would wear a uniform and walk into a school. The day when I would attend school like other children never came. I continued to work during the day and was homeschooled in the evening. While it was hard, I looked forward to the evenings of studying. Those few hours made me feel normal like the other kids. Days turned to months and months to years. Before I knew it, I was eligible to appear for the high school exams privately. I was beyond proud to finally receive my high school diploma. Years of hard work had finally culminated to this achievement. In my own little way, I felt accomplished.

We called Pakistan our home for nine years. In those nine years, we had numerous instances when we relocated because the Mujahedeen located us. Strangely, moving to a new home felt like second nature to us. In nine years, we had lived in every major city in Pakistan. Every city posed its own set of challenges and difficulties. In spite of being a teenager, I had worked and tended for my family most of my life. Through the years I had gone from selling eggs and potatoes at schoolyards to opening a vegetable shop. Unlike people my age who lived a carefree life, I had saved money and lived a calculated life to be able to finally own a business. While I was very proud of my accomplishments, I always felt sad when I reflected on the life I had lived. I did not know what it means to be a child, to make mistakes and to live a carefree life. I was a breadwinner for my family since I was nine years old. I had been doing this for so long, I did not know life without working and providing for others.

One day a glowing Agha Jan walked into our house with a paper in his hand. "We are relocating to Dubai, United Arab Emirates," Agha Jan told us. We were excited. After nine years of living in Pakistan and looking over our shoulder for Mujahedeen and their counterparts, we were moving to United Arab Emirates. When a glowing Agha Jan walked into our house with the news of relocation, I secretly hoped we were relocating to Afghanistan. Although the news was not exactly what I had hoped for, I was happy to move to a safer place than Pakistan. We were ready to be free in the true sense of the word. For nine years we were prisoners in our own home. We packed whatever little belongings we had accumulated in those nine years.

We first set foot in Dubai in 2001. Instantly I knew Dubai was going to change my life for the better. As we drove through Dubai, I remember seeing clean streets, tall buildings, big malls, and shopping markets around. Dubai, with its abundance of immigrants, felt like an exotic and beautiful land, exactly how I had imagined it to be. Several immigrants called Dubai home, forming seventy percent of the population. I did not know how to speak Arabic. I knew it did not matter because I knew how to speak Farsi, Pashto, Urdu, Hindi and English. As soon as we arrived in Dubai, one of my father's friends arranged an apartment for us. It was a modest apartment with a couple of bedrooms, but it was better and cleaner than any place in Pakistan we called home. Everywhere we turned, we saw signs of luxury. Bright lights, big shopping malls, fancy restaurants, and beautiful beaches reminded us of how unreachable the glitz and glamor was.

Dubai, with her bright lights and big buildings, was everything we had dreamed about, but never thought it would happen. We were in Dubai for couple of days when we realized how expensive basic items like onions and potatoes were. My father finally started working on his music career again. We as a family could not believe my father was singing again. My brother and I continued to provide for our family while my father worked on establishing himself once more. I wanted my other siblings to have a normal childhood. I wanted them to attend school unlike me.

My father's friend was looking for someone to oversee his import and export company. Since my father referred me, he decided to trust in me to oversee his company. After selling eggs, potatoes, and vegetables, I was ecstatic to finally oversee a company. On my first day, I realized the company was a one-man show. I had to take care of everything from clearing goods for customs and distributing to whole sellers, to taking care of imports coming in. He was impressed by my work and decided to let go of all the other employees. He did not allocate transportation expenses. Whenever I had to visit sites to clear goods, I walked miles to get one consignment cleared. I could not afford to spend money on taxis and buses when I had a family to feed at home. My priority was my sibling's education and I wanted to save every penny to pay for their school needs. My three younger brothers were accepted to expensive private schools. In Dubai, only Arabs were admitted to government school where the fees were waived. Immigrants like us were forced to attend private schools.

Dubai provided the much-needed financial break for us as a family. In addition to my job, my brother also found a decently paying job. Music echoed in our house again as my father started earning money from his singing. After months of saving, I finally bought a computer for myself. I had learned how to use a computer in Pakistan. I got an internet connection for my computer, which opened a new world for me. I was fascinated and felt empowered by the knowledge available at my fingertips. I spent hours searching for different things and quenching my thirst for knowledge. I also sneakily practiced my English skills.

I continued to be enamored by computers and the internet. On an unsuspecting day in 2003, I searched for Afghans online and stumbled upon an old childhood friend. I sent her an email and waited with baited breath to hear from her. I was thrilled to receive a response from her. We started conversing regularly online and later over the phone. During those conversations, I learned she had moved to California in America. We were both nineteen years old. She sent me her picture one day. I remember thinking she had grown into a beautiful girl. Beyond the physical beauty, I was very impressed by how she retained the Afghan culture, even in America. Through the many conversations we had, I began falling in love with her. After many sleepless nights, I professed my love to her. We had not met in person yet. She told me she respected my feelings, but love was a commitment of a lifetime for her. She wanted her first love to be the one she got married to. Although I reassured her of my intentions to make her my wife, she was not convinced.

The year was 2006. It had been three years since we started conversing with each other. She told me she was visiting Afghanistan with her mother. I decided to meet her in Afghanistan. America had defeated the Taliban government in Afghanistan and several Afghans were going back to visit the home they left behind. I had visited Afghanistan several times, but this time I was going to meet her. I met her for three minutes at her aunt's house in Kabul. It was not a society norm for a guy and a girl to meet before they are married. We exchanged pleasantries. I knew I wanted this girl to be mine forever. We kept in touch over the phone after I left her aunt's house. I met her a couple of times after that. I knew she was going to Dubai for two days before returning to America. I managed to book my return ticket on the same flight as hers. I knew I had to propose to her one more time. We boarded the flight to Dubai. I introduced myself to her mother and she instantly knew who I was from my father's name.

My father was at the airport to pick me up. I introduced my friend and her mother to him. I wanted my family to meet my future wife. Their meeting was short and sweet. Although my family insisted they stay with us during their time in Dubai, they decided to stay at the hotel. My father and I dropped them off at the hotel. On our way back home, my father's gaze told me he knew I was interested in that girl. He was not thrilled to have a daughter-in-law who was living in America. I told my mother and sisters about the guests who were coming home for lunch the next day. My friend and her mother came home upon my insistence and instantly everyone liked her. I was proud of my choice. I purchased a gold ring to propose when I dropped her at the airport. She didn't let me put the ring on her finger. She insisted if I wanted to marry her, I would have to ask for her hand in marriage through the families. I told her I loved her. She told me she knew and left. We continued to stay in touch while I worked on convincing my family to accept her. After three relentless years of convincing both sides, we decided to get engaged with their blessing. Finally I heard the three magical words: "I love you." I was ecstatic.

In 2009, I reached United States of America on a fiancé visa. The only force that brought me here was love. The journey to America was bittersweet, as I bid adieu to my family. I knew they no longer solely depended on me financially. My younger brother established his own business and my father's musical career had taken off. I owned a couple of shops in Dubai selling traditional Afghan clothing and accessories imported from Afghanistan and Pakistan at the Global Village market. For the first time in my young life, I had a sense of stability when I decided to immigrate to a new country. I left behind my family who I love dearly, the friends who I cherish immensely, and a business I had established with so much love.

I remember the day I landed in San Francisco airport. I had no idea what America would be like or how I would support myself. I packed my bags and made my way to America knowing I would survive. I remember the nine year old who was told, "There are people coming to take me away." I know if I could survive that day, I could survive it all. I went through two hours of the grueling immigration process. I was a Muslim Afghan man entering America post-9/11. I was repeatedly asked about my affiliation to any terrorist organization. I was in complete shock. I wondered why I would have anything to do with a terrorist organization. I felt unwelcome standing at San Francisco airport shielding a barrage of questions. I doubted my decision to come to America. I thought I would have to constantly prove my innocence.

I walked out of the airport and my fiancée was standing there with the brightest smile on her face waiting for me. I felt reassured of my decision. I felt the support she had always assured me before I decided to move to USA. We headed home to meet her family. On our way my fiancée informed me of the apartment she had rented for us to live in after our marriage. She did not want me to feel uncomfortable living with her family. I didn't know whether I was happy or sad to live away from family. I was raised in a big family with six siblings. I could not imagine not having the chaos of people around all the time. As I sat in the car being driven to meet her family I wondered how I would deal with living alone while she went to work as an engineer. I was almost certain the silence would kill me. I was assured I wouldn't last a week. I hid the fears I was feeling with a smile on my face. The dark clouds of loneliness were already engulfing my world and I had been in America for less than five hours.

America was almost synonymous with loneliness for me. I was alone in an empty apartment most of the day while my wife was at work. I had worked since I was nine; I counted the days of the week based on my work. I did not know me when I did not have a job. I was jobless and felt aimless. I did not know who I was anymore or what I wanted to do. I knew where my life was headed at nine when I was selling snacks to grade kids. Sitting in an empty apartment, I searched for an identity for the first time in my life. My wife suggested I continue my education at a community college. While it was something I had dreamed about for the longest, I was an Afghan man. It was a cultural taboo for a man to live off of his wife's income. I have always been the one who people relied on for support. I was not used to being supported by someone. The first year in America was very hard emotionally. I was completely depressed and lonely. We were a newly married couple. Instead of enjoying our marriage, my finances loomed like a dark cloud over me. I didn't want to go outside. I did not enjoy my marriage. I felt like a prisoner in my own house.

It had been a year since I had landed in America. My depression continued to spiral downwards. One day as I was lamenting on my situation,

I got an idea to start my own business selling Afghan traditional clothing and jewelry. I had all my contacts in Afghanistan and Pakistan. I connected with one of them with a plan to start a business in California. I had zero capital to invest since I had spent all the money I had saved on my wedding and surviving my first year in America. He decided to support me by providing me with the goods. The plan was to repay him as I sold them. I began working on my marketing strategy. I contacted my friend in Europe who offered to create a website for me. Again, I would pay him after I made money. Slowly, the pieces were falling in place. My depression was replaced by a new sense of achievement.

I did not know how much I could sell in America, but I believed in my hard work and dedication. I received my first shipment. In addition to the website, I started advertising my goods on all social media platforms. I had a mannequin I dressed up in different attires. I took pictures of the dresses and uploaded them on my website. I researched the market price, competitor's prices, and priced my goods accordingly. My aim was to sell better quality products at a cheaper price. I knew I would make lesser profit, but I also knew the quality would speak for itself.

It was 2am when I heard a notification on my cell phone. I was working on my website layout when I casually looked at the notification. I had received my first payment of $300 for two pairs of clothes. I was beyond excited. I woke my wife up as I showed her the notification. She couldn't believe it either. She was happy I had finally found a new hobby to keep myself occupied. My website started growing gradually. One order became two and before I knew it orders started pouring in. After four years of endless hard work, I am able to earn a decent income from my website. I thank God for it each day. As my income grew, I began enjoying America. After years in America, I started noticing the beauty of California with its wonderful weather all year round. I started enjoying my married life and appreciating my wife more. She had patiently waited while I transitioned into my American life.

Before I could enter America, I had complete confidence in my English skills. I thought I spoke decent English. The moment I landed here, I noticed people in America spoke too fast. Even after five years in America, I am still getting used to it. I have heard people in the South speak much slower than in California. I think I should invest in moving out there. Here in California, I have to ask people to repeat themselves frequently during conversations. In between all the depression and starting a business, I took my assessment test at a community college. I was accepted into college and started taking classes. The first day I went to college, I could feel the young nine-year-old me jumping inside. All my life I wanted to attend school in a classroom setting. I was finally living the moment I had been missing for so long. While going to college had been a dream come true, getting back to the habit of studying and staying focused has been hard. I am trying my best to juggle everything and will not give up. I have few more classes before I finish my business management degree.

Life in America has been good. I have a loving wife, a home, a car, and my own business. It has been extremely difficult to be away from friends and family. I had plenty of friends in Dubai. Some of them were Arabs who helped me converse fluently in Arabic. Every time I converse in Arabic here, I think about them. Simple everyday situations make me miss my family and friends. Initially when I came to America, I saw my wife as just my wife and missed having friends terribly. With time we forged a relationship beyond the husband and wife situation. I started seeing her as my friend, which made my life better.

Sometimes I reflect on the life I have lived. I remember my Agha Jan telling me there were people coming to take him away. I remember being scared as I walked the many miles to Ghazni with my uncle and family. I was nine years old then. Since those words changed my life, I have lived in Pakistan for nine years, called Dubai home for eight years, and have been living in America for six years now. I have lived outside of Afghanistan for the majority of my life. Yet, those nine years in Afghanistan have made an imprint in my life beyond anything I have experienced. Afghanistan is more than just the country of my ancestors. She is more than just the place I was born in. In spite of living outside of Afghanistan for the majority of my life, I feel a connection with Afghanistan that is inexplicable. It stems from my father's music I grew up hearing, the pride I feel as I walk the land of my forefathers, and a sense of being home in Afghanistan.

Are You Really Living in America?

I TOOK HIM IN MY ARMS for the first time. I have been in love, but this was beyond anything I had ever felt. For nine months, I had felt him in me, but watching him squirm in my arms made me feel love all over again. I watched him every second for the next few hours and smiled as he smiled in his sleep. He probably did not know, but I was so in love with him. I loved everything about him, his little face, his tiny little fingers, his cries, and his sleepy smiles. I tried to memorize every detail of this little person I had created and searched for myself in him. My world had changed in a second and we had gone from two to three. Yet, sitting in that hospital feeling the emotions of motherhood sweeping through my body, I felt lonely. I was used to being lonely and have felt it since I first got married years ago.

"Roselin, do you take this man to be your lawfully wedded husband?" I tried to sneak a look at the man standing next to me through the veil. I remember looking at myself in the mirror that morning and not recognizing the person looking back at me. She was beautiful with kohl-lined eyes, lipstick on her lips, and a glow on her face. My mother placed the veil on my head as my sister fixed the pleats of my white sari. Before long I was walking down the aisle with a man I had talked to for ten minutes before, that I am now supposedly taking as my husband. I coyly nodded my head and we were married. I was excited to be married, but I was even more excited to go on my honeymoon to Singapore and Thailand.

I had never traveled outside of India before my honeymoon. Singapore seemed like every big city in India, except it was much cleaner. I really liked Phuket, Thailand, with its caves and beautiful beaches, but it did not feel like a foreign country to me. In Singapore and Thailand I got to know the man I had married, but our honeymoon came to an end as we parted ways at the airport. He was going to the United States of America while I was going to wait for him in India.

I turned back to look at him as we parted ways. I felt a heart wrenching pain and already missed him terribly. Since my husband did not have a US citizenship, he could not bring his spouse with him to the United States of America. I had been preparing for this reality since we first got engaged. I tried everything from writing exams to joining Bible College that guaranteed an H1B work visa to the United States of America. Instead of dreaming of my fiancé, I was busily studying and dreaming of speaking American English as I trained for TOEFL (Training of English as a foreign Language). When every attempt to live together in the United States of America failed, we decided we were going to live apart. After a week together on our honeymoon, I returned back to India, and he returned to the United States of America. I lived for six months with my parents-in-law as a good bride. My father-in-law continued to follow me around and my over-protected life continued with my marriage.

"I am returning back to India. My company has allowed me to work from India."

I jumped around the house ecstatic. My husband was returning back to India and was going to work from here. He would work nights because of the time difference, while we would live together. Initially it was exciting, but with time my husband found it challenging to attend meetings in the US from India. After two years of living in India and working nights, we decided to immigrate to Canada. My husband's job in America let him work from Canada, so we were moving to Vancouver.

I was standing at the airport waiting for my flight to Vancouver, Canada. I had prepared for this journey since the day I spoke to my husband for ten minutes. I dreamt of building a life with him in America. We had dreamt of making this trip since the day I got engaged to him. Yet, standing at the airport holding a boarding pass that read "Vancouver" two years later felt unreal. Two years of endless disappointments, trials, tribulations, and several shattered dreams had culminated to this moment in our life. After two years, we boarded our flight to Vancouver, Canada.

In 2007, my husband and I walked out of our flight into Vancouver International Airport in Canada. When I left India, I thought Vancouver would be similar to Singapore and Thailand. I had more preconceived notions when I was visiting Singapore for my honeymoon. I was told the beauty of Singapore was unparalleled since it was one of the most beautiful places to visit. I knew it was very clean, having heard stories of not being able to chew gum. I should have been impressed considering it was my first trip outside of India, but I was not too impressed. Thailand was pretty, but not impressive either. If one of the most beautiful places to visit did not impress me, how would Vancouver be any different? I knew I was wrong when I stepped outside the airport on my way to our hotel. The beauty of Vancouver bowled me over and I was swept off my feet by the natural beauty of the place. I strained my neck trying to see all the beauty around me and was mesmerized. This was the most beautiful place I had visited and I could not wait to begin our life here.

The cab drove through the beautiful streets to a high-rise hotel in downtown Vancouver. I opened the curtains and caught a glimpse of the city in all her glory. I knew at that moment I was in Canada, miles away from the small South Indian city of Tamil Nadu I had called home. As breathtaking as the landscape around was, I felt pangs of loneliness as I missed my mom, family, and the familiar sounds and smells of home. I received my green card in Canada, making this move more permanent and concrete. While living in Canada, my husband applied for my United States green card as soon as he became a US citizen. He continued to travel between United States and Canada, while I stayed at home in my plush apartment in downtown Vancouver, pondering where my life was headed. Every Indian person I met was a computer engineer, IT engineer, or had a Master's in computers. I was neither of those. I began researching on careers in Vancouver for non-engineering Indians and decided to pursue a diploma in Montessori. I really enjoyed my first Montessori course. The prospect of being an on-call substitute kindergarten teacher made the diploma very appealing. I felt accomplished.

While studying as a student, I decided to work part time elsewhere. Most days I was alone in my downtown Vancouver apartment. In spite of attending Montessori classes, I was depressed every time I walked into my empty apartment. I turned on soap operas to drown the silence around me, but it made me feel lonelier. I looked around our apartment complex for part time work and stumbled upon a bakery looking for help. I dialed the number with confidence. A lady answered the phone introducing herself as Tina. She explained what she was looking for and asked if I could come in for an interview. I should have been excited, but I wasn't. Although I decided to go in for the interview, I had no idea what Tina the white woman was going to ask me. I had arrived in Vancouver not too long ago and had never talked to a white person before. I felt my confidence melt away, but I decided to interview with her for the experience. I walked into the bakery looking for Tina the white lady, but she turned out to be Asian. I was confused how she could be Tina. All Asians I knew back home from movies had very difficult names. She told me her name was Shu Ching something and Tina was her American name. Tina hired me and I was excited. The next morning I walked into the bakery for my first day at work. She walked me through the menu with items named espresso, cappuccino, etc. I did not know what those words meant. I saw people sit around and eat snacks so I thought maybe cappuccino, espresso, and latte were snacks to be had with coffee. It took me a whole day before I knew those were different kinds of coffee. She did a coffee recipe dump on me while I stood there perplexed and confused. The coffee shop helped me get over my loneliness. I met people who hung out at the coffee shop for relaxation. During one of my conversations with a coworker, he told me how his husband was at home on that specific day. I tried to remember if he said husband. I told myself it was my language barrier that made wife sound like husband. Why would a man have a husband? The only logical explanation was I misheard him. Tina told me two weeks later he was gay and explained what it was. I was introduced to the word "gay."

I completed my Montessori course and received my diploma. I was an on-call substitute teacher at a kindergarten. It was my first day at school as I walked in chirpy and excited. I was watching children play when the head teacher said, "Roselin, can you please check on Sarah? She had an accident." "Accident!" I exclaimed, as I ran to check on Sarah in true Bollywood style. I ran all the possibilities in my head by the time I reached Sarah. She might have fainted and hit her head, I hope she did not lose a lot of blood, another child could have hit her...the possibilities were endless. I reached Sarah and wondered why she looked fine for someone who had an accident. I checked her head while asking her if she was in pain when the other assistant teacher told me Sarah had an accident in her diapers. She needed a diaper change. I was embarrassed. In India, when we use the word accident it meant blood, broken bones, and even death, but never a diaper change. During one of our playtimes, the head teacher asked me to scoot back while I stood there with no idea what scoot back meant until she used move back. I repeated scoot back in my head repeatedly until it became part of my everyday language.

My husband took me to visit Niagara Falls on a warm fall morning.

He pointed to the other side of the falls and told me "You see that side. That is the United States of America." America seemed liked a distant, unattainable land. We continued our quest to immigrate to the US. In 2009, my husband became a US citizen and he filed for my green card. My husband traveled between America, Canada, and India a lot during our time in Canada. While filling my green card paperwork, he filled in the wrong dates for which we were rejected. The American dream continued to elude us. We tried redoing all the paperwork again, but this time we were accepted. We moved to United States of America from Canada. It was a dream come true for us.

When I came to Vancouver, I did not have any preconceived notions. I did not know of anyone who lived there, but America was different. I had watched America from a distance through the movie screen and sometimes by imagining an America through the stories people told of people they knew who lived in America. I felt ready to finally have my American moment. I imagined an exotic America as pretty as the Canadian landscape. We initially lived in Palo Alto, California. Palo Alto, I was told, was home to the rich people who founded Apple and Google. It had an ambience of richness with beautiful houses everywhere. We eventually moved from Palo Alto to Fremont, California, shattering my illusion of America. Fremont was different from Palo Alto. Fremont reminded me of India each time I walked in my apartment building. The air smelled of home cooked Indian food, recalling summers in India. It should have made me happy. Instead, I felt cheated of the American moment I wanted to live every day. I'd rather be in India if I were to live in a place that felt like India. Vancouver introduced me to a new world filled with exotic food like Thai, Mexican, and Chinese. When we moved to Fremont, California, there were an abundance of Indian restaurants around our neighborhood. Each time we went out to eat, it was always Indian food. We were officially in the United States of India.

On a warm summer morning I sat in my bathroom nervous and scared. I stared at the pregnancy test I had just taken, while waiting for the results. I saw the two lines appear on the pregnancy stick. I was pregnant. After almost eight years of marriage, I was finally on my way to motherhood. We had called America home for two years by then. I had continued my Montessori career and was rather happy in my space. Yet, those two lines on that pregnancy stick rocked my world. I walked into my Montessori school the next day and quit my job. As a child growing up in India, I remember my mother being at my beck and call. I knew I wanted that for my child. My husband was earning enough for me to be a stay at home mother. During the nine months of my pregnancy, I ate healthy and kept myself stress free and happy. I read how my stress would reflect on my baby, so I kept myself happy. My husband did not want to bring either of our parents here for my delivery, although I wanted my mother for moral support. I ate well, slept well, and prayed. I was lonely. My friend helped us by cooking healthy food for me. She took care of my needs throughout my pregnancy. A few weeks before my due date, she had an accident and broke her wrist. Suddenly I was alone again. My husband decided to bring my in-laws to America to help us with the baby.

I woke up and realized my water had broken. We rushed to the hospital and before I knew it I was holding him in my arms. I looked at him as he lay on my chest. I could not believe he was mine. I tried to memorize every detail about him: his little fingers, closed eyes, and the smell of his body. My whole life flashed before my eyes as I watched him sleep. We decided to name him Roy. My in-laws reached the United States of America four days after Roy's birth. I had my husband, in-laws, and my little baby with me. In spite of all the chaos around me, I missed my mother a lot. I bottled up all the emotions I felt while taking care of my baby. Before long, my in-laws returned back to India and my mother came to America. She was an immense support for me. My mother helped me with my postpartum depression and helped me calm down. When Roy turned seven months old, I put him in swimming class. I wanted to enforce one activity at a time for him. I continued to experience postpartum depression. The routine of breastfeeding him, changing his diapers, and feeding him made me lonely. I decided to take classes like sign language to help me break the routine.

Raising Roy in America has been a challenge for me. Even though I am married, I sometimes feel like a single mother. My husband is busy with his work and I am alone at home with Roy. I struggled to understand why he cried sometimes. Although my in-laws and my mother were here for support, they were scared to give me suggestions. Had I raised my child in India, our parents would have helped me by suggesting herbal cures for his illnesses like stomach pain. The doctors in India prescribe exactly what you need to do when your child is sick. In America, doctors give you choices and as parents you have to choose. It was overwhelming for us since this was our first child. I also noticed I am overprotective of my child in comparison to how I was raised. I remember growing up in India and being able to run outside with my cousins. My grandparents took us around while our parents stayed home. Here, I do not let Roy away from my sight. Although his umbilical cord was severed the day I gave birth to him, I have an imaginary umbilical cord connected to my baby and his every move.

When I got pregnant I convinced my husband to sell our television. I had read in the American Pediatrics book, as well as in my Montessori training, that children get addicted to television at a young age. I also refused to give my son baby food or kids' meals. When we started feeding him solid food, I packed food wherever we went, even if it was Target or Costco. I knew exactly what my child was eating and it gave me a sense of relief. We refuse to give my son juice or sugary drinks. I explained the difference between chocolates and candy and told him he could eat chocolates but no candy. I breastfed my child until he was two years old. When he turned two, we went to our doctor to stop breast-feeding him. The doctors told me about a cold turkey treatment wherein I stop feeding him. Even if he cries I was not supposed to breastfeed him. It was easier said than done. I tried the cold turkey treatment. Each time I carried him when he cried for milk, he automatically grabbed my breasts. It was hard for me while my husband thought it should be easy. He insisted I follow the cold turkey treatment. I was not made for cold turkey treatment. I decided to visit India to stop breast-feeding. In India, my mother made a Neem paste and rubbed it on my breasts. Neem leaves have a bitter taste and when I breastfed him he did not like the taste of Neem leaves. Slowly, he stopped wanting breast milk. My mother carried him when he got cranky for the milk, supporting me while I stopped breastfeeding.

I visited India several times during the seven years I have lived outside of India. Each time I go back, I reminisce of the life I once had. My mother cooks my favorite meals and I become the baby of my house again. My last trip to India, I went to a party at my in-laws. I was meeting my husband's cousin who was very close to me. She hugged me and said "Akka (sister), you haven't changed at all. Are you really living in America?" I had lived in America and Canada for seven years at that point. I thought I had changed a lot since I lived here. My English has improved for the better and I understand the American slang better. Yet, she thought I did not change. I looked at myself in the mirror and the girl looking back at me was the same girl who lived in India. She had gone from wearing salwar kameez and saree to jeans, but her hair continues to reach her lower back with no style. The girl looking back at me might have become a mother and wife in America, but she was the jeans-clad Indian me. I returned back to America and instantly decided

I was going to change myself. I was on the threshold of turning forty and I had to change before that milestone. I cut my hair multiple times until it reached few inches below my shoulder. Initially I did not like it, but with time I began developing an interest in fashion. I started wearing dresses. I wanted to make sure next time I visit India, no one would doubt my American stay.

I watch Roy growing up in America and wonder if I have instilled our culture in him. I try hard each day to make sure he understands who he is and where he is from. As he started attending preschool, I noticed his fluency in English. I speak good English, but find it difficult to talk in English at home. I am a South Indian Tamilian born and raised in India and Tamil is a part of my soul and identity. When Roy speaks in English, my husband and I respond in Tamil. Each time I hear him babble and talk in Tamil, I feel emotions beyond pride. I continue to feel the pressures of American culture, even after seven years in America. I find myself being singled out because I don't like pizza, which is considered good food here. I find myself being stared at for not owning a television.

It's been seven years since I walked into the airport on my way to Canada. I remember I was overwhelmed with emotions. I was sad to leave my family behind, but I was also excited to finally come to Canada. I had several dreams - dreams of a beautiful life with my husband. We have since that day gone from two to three with Roy being the most beautiful part of this journey. While the years have been beautiful and exciting, it has also been very lonely. Family means everything to me and each time I visit India I am reminded of everything I have missed. I see the graying hair on my mom's head and realize the time that sped by me. I see the passage of time in my nieces and nephews; I see the passage of time in the wrinkles on my sister's face and wonder where the time has disappeared. Some time in the next few years, my family and I will relocate to India, bidding adieu to the years of loneliness I have felt here.

The journey has been comfortable and filled with luxury. Our house reminds me of the successful life we have built in America. I have gone from the overprotected girl who went everywhere with her parents and in-laws to a confident woman who drives herself around. We have cars, a beautiful house, nights out in restaurants - but I would trade everything for my life in India, where I was surrounded by family and love. The hair might have become shorter, the jeans might have replaced the sari in my world, but India remains the only place I call my home. India continues to be the only place this South Indian girl from Tamil Nadu really belongs.

Kosovo? Really...Cool!

I AM EIGHTEEN YEARS OLD, white, and European. My country is younger than I am, having received independence in 2008. I am not from London, Paris, or even Croatia. My country is a speck in the glittering continent of Europe. It is called Kosovo. The small cities in Italy and France are known around the world, but my state Kosovo is hardly heard of. I did not experience the Kosovo war of 1998-1999, but I have grown up hearing stories from my family. In 2008, we finally got our independence from Serbia, ending years of inter- ethnic commotions. I did not know a life outside of Kosovo, yet growing up I had big dreams of coming to America. I was aware of the American influence on Kosovo while growing up there. The Albanians (Kosovo people are called Albanians) might not know English, but they knew of Bill Clinton, the US, and using "thank you" as a term. Bill Clinton was a big celebrity in Kosovo, with Bill Clinton Boulevard being the main street connecting Pristina, our capital, to the airport. America loomed over my life while growing up in Kosovo. I knew I wanted to live in America even as a teenager. I dreamed about coming to America for high school. It never happened, but in 2014 I got my American visa to attend college. I was ecstatic and, in August 2014, I boarded my flight from Kosovo to Atlanta.

The date was August 8th, 2014. I arrived at Atlanta Hartsfield Airport after boarding three different flights. It was a long journey from Kosovo to Atlanta. I had been waiting to visit America for as long as I can remember. Even in Kosovo we had heard about America being the land of opportunities. I knew I could be successful in a place like America. When it was time to board my flight to America, I felt a surge of emotions. It was my first flight. I was traveling alone without any family or friends, which made the journey so much more terrifying. I was the first person to move to America in my family. As my family members battled their individual emotions, I felt a mixture of happiness, excitement, curiosity, nervousness, and intense anxiety as I boarded my first flight. I was traveling on an uncharted path. Airports were unfamiliar and I often followed other people hoping I was following protocol. The three connecting flights did not help my situation. I was stressed out through the entire journey, praying I would somehow reach my destination safely. I second-guessed my decision as I battled anxiety and loneliness through the entire flight ride. I felt validated when I heard the immigration officer at Atlanta airport greet me with the line, "Welcome to the United States of America." I felt a surge of emotions washing through my body. I was nervous and excited.

Growing up in Kosovo, I had an image of America. I knew America was bigger than Kosovo, but walking out of Atlanta airport I realized America was much bigger than what I expected. Even Atlanta airport seemed bigger than any other airport I had been in. As I walked through the airport I saw diversity I had never experienced. Kosovo was comprised of white Albanian people and I was only used to seeing white people everywhere. America welcomed me with a fashion show of diversity as African Americans, Asians, Latinos and white people surrounded me. I was experiencing the melting pot culture I had heard about in my first thirty minutes in America. I stood there, amazed by the mini world I was part of, as I saw people from every corner of the world walk around me. While diversity welcomed me, I was introduced to the harsh realities of America instantly. I did not know racism and prejudice continued to exist in America. I arrived in 2014 when the protests of Ferguson and other killings of black people by whites were always in the news. It shocked me to know racism continued to exist in America. I was walking in Atlanta when I first saw a homeless man holding a sign for help. I was shocked to see poverty and poor people in America. I grew up thinking there was no poverty in America and everyone was rich. I was saddened to know there were plenty of homeless and poor people who could barely eat. My ideal image of America was crushed within the first few days of being in America.

As I acquainted myself with Atlanta and America, I realized how different my life had been in Kosovo. Even as a child in Kosovo I knew I did not belong there. I knew Kosovo was the kind of place one retired in. I was determined to live the kind of life I dreamt about and knew then I had to leave Kosovo. It was hard to find a good job and the ones you found ended up being low paying jobs. Life was interesting and challenging in Kosovo. Most cities were compressed and centralized, which made it easier to walk to different places rather than driving a car. Families lived close to each other and relatives met each other weekly. Even during my initial days in America I realized relatives rarely met each other here. My friends here told me they met family on days like Thanksgiving for meals. I found that very different to my life in Kosovo, where my relatives visited each other weekly. I came from a big family and was often surrounded by loved ones. I also grew up in a micro society where everyone knew each other. I found it extremely hard to transition from the micro society setting to the American lifestyle. Something as simple as driving a car as a necessity was new to me. People in Kosovo drove cars because they liked driving and not because they had to drive around. I realized I could not do anything without a car in America. Kosovo is a farming culture where all food is grown locally. The farmers do not know how to modify the produce for profits. The first time I ate in America, I realized the food was highly processed and genetically modified. Even vegetables I ate all my life tasted different in the United States than in Kosovo.

Weeks went by and before I knew it was time to make my college debut. I don't remember being this scared and nervous in my entire life as I was on my first day in college. I walked into my college campus and the diversity startled me. I had been in America for a few weeks by then but still seeing so many different people together in one place made me very nervous. There were people from different races, cultures, ethnicities and religions in my college. I was further reminded of the mini world melting pot American culture. I felt very isolated and lonely. Nobody talked to me on campus. People already knew each other and stayed with one another. I was reminded of my loneliness during the initial college days. I stayed to myself and rarely mingled with others. I am a computer science major and the benefits of being in a technology field included meeting other international immigrants like myself. We bonded over our mutual experiences in America and the loneliness we felt living here. With time, we started hanging out and exploring America together. I went from dreading going to college in fear of the loneliness to looking forward to college. University started feeling like home and I started enjoying my American journey. Each day made me feel better than the day before.

While making friends has been challenging, my name has posed its own set of challenges. It was my first day at college and most of the professors take roll to ensure they have space for waiting students to enroll. It was my first class in college and in America. I did not know how I was supposed to respond to my name and paid attention to how the students prior to me responded. Although my last name started with an A, there were few students ahead of me in roll call. When called upon by the professor, they responded with, "Here," and I memorized it. I waited for my professor to call my name but what followed was a shadow of my name,

Lisian. I corrected my professor, but he almost always seemed to have a problem with my name. It has been a problem during my entire stay in America. I hate introducing my name to new people as no one can pronounce it correctly. In Kosovo, alphabets are pronounced differently when compared to English. For example, L, which is the first letter of my name, is pronounced the same way as in Spanish and double L "Ll" is pronounced as English L. I am yet to find an American who pronounces my name correctly, but Spanish people do more justice to my name. After months of dealing with various pronunciations of my name from Lyesian to Lis-ian, I shortened my name to Lisi for some of my friends. I am yet to publicize my nickname to everyone else.

It was my first week in college and I was talking to one of my classmates when he asked me, "Where are you originally from?" I proudly replied, "Kosovo." He looked perplexed, almost contemplating what his response ought to be. After few seconds of awkward silence he replied, "Really? Cool!" I did not know what that answer meant, but when this reaction continued each time I told people I am from Kosovo, I realized people had no idea where this place was. I lived in Kosovo my entire life and never realized how unknown my part of the world was until I started living in the US. After months of dealing with perplexed reactions, I started saying I am Albanian. It makes it easier on the people who want to know where I am from and it makes it easier for me.

Although my English was not American, I had immense confidence in my English speaking skills. I was not worried about the communication aspect when I decided to move to America for college. I could understand American movies and TV shows while in Kosovo. I believed I was prepared until I landed in America. I live in Georgia, where people have strong and deep southern accent. I had never heard southern American English before I landed in Georgia. I struggled and continue to struggle with the southern accent. I often find myself asking people to repeat while talking to them. I had several preconceived notions about America. I thought everyone was rich, there was no poverty, and no racism. I also expected things would be more expensive than in Kosovo. They paid more than Kosovo, so I expected things to be expensive. I knew things would be expensive, but I never expected it to be so expensive. I got my first heart attack when I saw how expensive university fees were. I was told then it was because I was a foreign student and residents paid less. It made logical sense to me then, although it did hurt to pay so much money. The first time I saw the bill at a restaurant I ate, it baffled me to no end. I could not believe it could be almost $20 for one person. Food was at least three times more expensive than in Kosovo - and the food was processed, too. I told myself it included processing fee since food was processed and genetically modified in America. I could not justify the price on car insurance though. Car insurance in America was almost seven times more than what it was in Kosovo. I am amazed at the number of cars I see on streets here in spite of the expensive car insurance. I am hoping someday after I get my degree I will feel less pain while going to a restaurant or purchasing car insurance. Someday when I see my paycheck the numbers, will tally out and make sense to this Kosovo boy.

As I already mentioned, the restaurant bill is often too high for a foreign college student like myself. When I first reached America, I was eager to eat at different restaurants. The more I saw the money I was spending on food, the lesser the urge became. Eventually I started choosing fast food over non-fast food places. I visited a fast food joint with some of my friends after college one day. I had by then made some American and international friends. I walked into the restaurant and took a seat by the window. I was waiting for the waiter to come take my order. I enjoyed the view and with time I started getting restless. I wondered why my friends weren't sitting with me but standing in a long line.

My friend walked up to me and asked me what I was doing sitting down. I told him I was waiting for the waiter to come take my order. He burst out laughing and said, "Dude, this is a fast food joint. It is self-service. You will be waiting here all day if you are hoping for someone to take your order." I felt so stupid sitting there and was really embarrassed. He continued laughing for a while, after which I embarrassingly told him in Kosovo we sat down and waited for the waiter to take our order. He then brought our food to us.

As a kid growing up in Kosovo I had a dream, a dream that made me travel miles away from my family to America. I wanted to live in the arc lights of the big city, make money, and succeed in my career. I wanted to live the American dream. I left Kosovo for a more comfortable life in America, yet there are so many things I miss about Kosovo. I miss the comforts of my home, my family, friends, and food. I have not gone back to Kosovo since I came to America, but I hope to visit them sometime in the end of 2015. I have been in America for less than a year now and, yet, it feels like home. Although I was born and raised in Kosovo, I always felt I did not belong there. I felt I needed to chase the arc lights of the big city by myself. I always knew I wanted to leave Kosovo for a journey of self-discovery. When I left Kosovo, I was going to America to discover myself and I do not regret a second of it. It has been hard and lonely, but it has also been exciting. I will probably live in America for the rest of my life. For the first time in eighteen years, I have started feeling like I belong. I have started feeling I am finally home.

I Am Exotic, Mocha P-Diddy!

IT FELT LIKE EVERY OTHER DAY as I walked the hallways of my school in Pune, India. Since the last few days, I had started feeling different. While most of my friends talked about girls, I was noticing the boys around me. I noticed the smile on their faces, their twinkling eyes, and felt drawn towards the boys in my class. Initially it did not bother me, but the longer I hung out with my friends the more I realized it was not "normal" behavior. My friends hung out in the school hallways looking at girls, talking about them, and noticing their every movement. None of them noticed the boys around them but me. I hung out with my friends and forced myself to talk about girls so no one would notice the difference in me. I pretended to be like them, although I knew I was different. I was confused. All through fifth standard I pretended to like girls.

I lie in bed staring at the ceiling fan above me. I could not sleep. I could hear the commotion from the living room as my parents packed our suitcases. We as a family were moving to Texas, America, and I was going to attend sixth standard in the United States. I was scared, nervous, and anxious hoping I could fit in. Texas has taken over my thoughts and the confusions from fifth grade had disappeared into oblivion.

"Welcome to the United States of America," the immigration authority said as he handed us our papers. A gamut of emotions ran through my head. I felt nervous, anxious, homesick, and excited as I walked through Texas airport. I looked around for any confirmation of being in America.

The America I had envisioned through the many movies I watched as a kid in India had tall buildings, white people, big companies, money, and fast cars. As I walked through Texas airport, I saw white people around me and knew I was in America. As an eleven year old, my life had gone from living in India to walking through the gates of America in the blink of my eye and I tried to soak it all in.

I was starting sixth grade in the United States of America. In India we called it sixth standard, but I coached myself to say grade and not standard. I went to school with my bag full of books, and instantly noticed there was hardly anybody like me. In a school full of mostly Caucasian kids, I was among the four or five brown kids in the entire school. I was the only non-Caucasian kid in most of my classes in sixth grade. I was overwhelmed and tried hard to fit in. Since I wasn't born in America, I did not know how to fit in and look like the rest of the kids. Yet at eleven years of age, all I wanted was to be like everyone else. I did not want to be different or exotic. On a warm summer day I decided to wear shorts to school like the rest of the boys. I wore my best pair of shorts and walked into my class confidently. As I walked through the room, I felt girls follow me with their eyes. I felt validated with all the attention I was receiving until someone called my shorts girly. I knew then the eyes followed me because I looked different and not because I looked like everyone else. In India, boys in sixth grade wore shorts that were above the knee. In the United States of America, boys wore shorts which were below the knee. Shorts above the knee were considered girly.

On my first day of school, I walked between the students in class to introduce myself to the teacher. I practiced my introduction in my head as I walked the walk. I shyly said, "My name is Parag," in thick Indian-accented English. My teacher did a double take trying to pronounce Parag. Each time I taught people how to pronounce my name correctly, but it almost always ended up sounding like Prague. So with time I Americanized my name to Prague. My introductions have changed from, "My name is Parag," to, "I am Prague, like the city." Before I could become Prague, I was called P-rag, Payrag and, in some instances, P-Diddy jokingly. Initially I wondered who P-Diddy was and how my name became P-Diddy. P-rag sounded closer to my name than P-Diddy. Now that I am acquainted with P-Diddy through his music, I am glad to be the exotic mocha P-Diddy!

As an eleven year old, America was taking me through a whirlwind every day. I grappled trying to survive the changes and fit in among my Caucasian peers. Growing up in India offered different challenges in comparison to America. Children in Indian schools never bullied their peers irrespective of the differences. On the contrary, a Caucasian kid in an Indian school would be the most popular kid on campus. People are often heckled in college as a customary passage to adulthood and no one was spared. During one of my sixth grade days, I was walking to my choir class when I noticed three Caucasian boys following me. The average Caucasian kid is bigger in comparison to the average Indian kid and these boys were towering over me. Initially I heard them taunting me and before I knew it someone kicked me from behind. As I went down, I heard one of the boys call me "Sand Nigga." In India, Africans are referred to as Negroes and it is not considered a racist slur. I did not know it was racist at that time or what it meant. I limped to class in pain and explained the incident to my choir teacher. She stayed silent, but took me to the principal's office. They took actions on the boy who used the racist slur on me. Although I did not know it was racially charged, I was traumatized by that incident.

As the year came to an end, my family and I bid adieu to Texas and America. My one-year stint in America opened a new world, a more accepting world than I was used to. During my sixth grade in America, I noticed boys who were more open to liking other boys. There were boys in school who were more flamboyant, flashy, and rather feminine. My ignorance prompted me to assume they probably liked boys too because they were feminine. I still felt different and did not know why I felt different.

In spite of the whirlwind experiences in America, the country continued to intrigue us. We decided to move permanently to California in 2001. It was a more conscious decision this time around and we knew it was going to be for more than just a year. California was very different in comparison to Texas in the 1990's. California was more culturally and ethnically diverse than Texas. I was starting high school in California and could not attend the first day of school. I had to get a TB test, which is mandatory for most schools and colleges. Unfortunately I tested positive for tuberculosis. After a grueling few hours of uncertainty and a chest X- RAY later, it was determined the TB test was positive because of a MMR (Mumps, Measles and Rubella) vaccine I was administered as a child in India. On the second day of school I wore my best outfit and my hair was parted perfectly with oil. I walked through the hallways confidently with my bag and hands full of books. My first class was geography and my teacher was named John Nix. Mr. Nix was very welcoming and instantly made me feel at ease. My confidence skyrocketed because of Mr. Nix and he became my mentor. Before I met Mr. Nix, I was an introvert who was extremely nervous about fitting in.

The move to California was easier on me than the initial Texas move. I was older, matured, and more equipped to deal with the cultural change than I was at eleven. The burgers, pizzas with extra cheese, and chocolates made perfect allies to my American journey and I devoured every single one of them. As I maneuvered my way through high school and America, my weight began to increase. I was 5'5 and still proudly carried my baby weight when I first moved to California. A few years later, my height shot up to 5'9-5'10, but so did my weight. I was never bullied or harassed because of my weight, so it never bothered me. When I started college at UC Davis, I stayed away from home for the first time in my life. I was around people who worked out every day, cared about their appearance, and lived a healthy lifestyle. I began inculcating some of those habits as I began eating healthy, working out, and trying to lose weight. Eventually I began eating only half a sandwich a day, running, and working out. As the pounds dropped, the more I starved myself of food. My self-confidence began to grow as I started making changes to my appearance. My oiled hair was replaced by gelled hair as my fashion sense evolved into hip and happening.

I traveled across continents before finally deciding to call America home. The ten-year-old fifth grader in India grew and matured into a man in California. The attraction I felt towards boys at ten continued to grow in me. I was perplexed initially and tried to ignore it. While Texas introduced me to a more accepting America, California introduced me to the word "gay." As I continued my American journey, I began accepting myself for who I was. I realized it was not going to change overnight and, if given a chance, I would not want it to change. After years of being confused and ignorant, I finally felt at peace with myself. It was still my little secret.

I continued living life with my secret all through college. Although I accepted myself, I did not come out of the closet in the true sense. After graduating from UC Davis, I started taking badminton classes at a gym. During the badminton class, I got to know a guy I had a crush on for the longest time in college. For the first time in my life, I was mentally, emotionally, and physically attracted to someone. I was perplexed on where to go from here. I knew it was time to come out of my shell. During one of my drunken moments, I sent a text message to my friend that read, "I have something to tell you. Please don't be mad at me. I want to be open with my friend. I don't want to hide an important part of myself with the people I am close to. I have known this for a while. I am gay." I waited with baited breath for her response. As I sat there staring at my phone, I was scared and nervous. Although I did not want to lose any of my friends over this, my biggest fear was being treated differently. I did not want anyone to be my friend while gossiping about me behind my back. As I sat there grappling with my thoughts, she sent me a text that read, "Parag, I am so glad you decided to share your secret with me. I want you to be honest with yourself. I support you in this and I feel special you decided to share this with me." She accepted me and supported me in my decision. We met few days later and she hugged me tight when she first saw me. I felt her support in her hug and I felt the validation I was looking for. After I came out to her, the process became easy. I started coming out to my other friends and all of them echoed the same sentiment: "We want you to be happy." The support was overwhelming. After coming out to some people, I had a successful recipe to coming out. Before I told people I was gay, I asked them of their opinion on my sexuality. Some acknowledged they knew all along, while the others were surprised.

While in high school during a casual afternoon, my mom calmly asked me "Are you gay?" I was jolted by that question. I wanted to be truthful with her, but had not acknowledged it to myself yet. I chickened out, looked down, and said, "No, I am not." I wish I had said yes. While I had cracked the coming out code, I had not come out to anyone in my family. I pondered on how I wanted to do it. I guess I could have used Google, but I chose alcohol power instead. On a drunken night, I decided to come out to my sister. My sister and I have been very close since childhood. I sent her a text message that read, "I have something to tell you. Please don't be mad at me. I have known this for a while. I am gay." My sister was shocked and worried how our parents would take it. A day later she came over to talk to me and was genuinely distraught. She was crying as she asked me if I was sure I was gay. I could not stand to see my sister crying, but I had to be strong. I told her I have known it for a while now. I was perplexed by her, "Are you sure?" question. It was not Halloween or April Fool's to be joking with her. I did not wake up with an epiphany that I was gay. I knew it since I was ten years old. I might not have known the term, but I knew what I was. She would always be my sister, but if she could not accept me for who I am, I could not be close with her. A few days later my sister talked to me again. She apologized for acting the way she did and told me she accepted and supported me. I always knew my sister would accept me, but I thought it would take her a month or so to accept me. I was surprised at how quickly she accepted me.

Every time my family and I decide to go back to India, I am excited for weeks before the actual trip. Although I battle allergies from the pollution, I am completely rejuvenated by my trip back home. I relive moments of my childhood with my friends and family. I have called America home for the past twelve years. When we first came to America, I was anxious and nervous about fitting in. It has taken years before I could completely adapt to this culture. Something as simple as fashion has been a challenge for an immigrant like me. I have had to hone my English skills although I spoke good English before. I had to Americanize it. I have had to Americanize my fashion and appearance, yet I carry a picture of that oiled hair high school boy in my pocket. It reminds me of my journey in America and the struggles to fit in.

Every time I think about home, I am conflicted on which is home. Ten years back if someone has asked me where was home, I would have said India in the blink of an eye. India was home and I missed everything about it. I missed my family, the familiar streets, the memories, and my friends. Everything in America was new and strange. In the years, I have transformed from a young boy to a man in America, especially in California. California has gone from strange to familiar, new memories have been formed along the way, and I have developed a sense of belonging here. I came to America as a confused boy with no sense of identity. America welcomed and accepted me, nurtured me as I entered manhood, and along the way made me the person I am today. When I came to America, I did not know if it would ever become home. I knew I would feel at home because my family was here with me, but doubted being at home here. America nurtured and transformed me. It became home. India continues to be my homeland, the place of my birth and the place I share cultural feelings with. America, specifically California, has become home and will always be home no matter where the journey takes me.

Daddy, I Want to be a Farmer One Day!

I REMEMBER THE MOMENT I carried my son for the first time in the hospital. He was a few minutes old. I watched this little person I had created in disbelief. I was a new father and I felt emotions beyond anything I had experienced in those few minutes when I held him in my hands. It has been a few years since that moment, yet I watch my son in disbelief to this day and cannot believe how fast he is growing up. I watch him babbling in Spanish and English, embracing his roots as he devours Mexican food with ease. He is the first generation Mexican American in our family. When I first carried him, I knew I wanted him to know his background, his culture, and his language. Every time I watch him flaunt our culture, I reminisce about my journey from Jalisco, Mexico, to America.

I was born in Jalisco, a very small farming town about an hour and half south of Guadalajara in Mexico. My town was so small that we joked if you blink your eye while driving, you might drive right past it. I am not sure how many people lived in Jalisco, but I know it was small. My parents were born in Mexico in two different small towns five minutes apart from each other. They came to the United States when they were in their twenties. I was two years old then. We moved from Jalisco, Mexico, to Oakland, California. We stayed in Oakland until I was in elementary school when we decided to move back to Mexico. I don't remember much about my initial days in Oakland. We moved back to Mexico when

I was in elementary school and stayed there until I completed three years of high school when we moved back to Oakland again.

I remember the first time my dad told us we were moving back to Mexico. I remember his exact words in Spanish, "Francisco, we are moving to Mexico," he said. I was six or seven years old then. I looked at him wide eyed. I loved Mexico and I believed moving to Mexico would be one big vacation. We often went back to Mexico for vacations and I loved spending time there. I expected every day in Mexico to be like my vacation days there surrounded by cousins and family. I did not realize it would be different until I started living there. It was a struggle for me to adapt to the lifestyle. My days were filled with chores and work that needed to be done from dawn to dusk. In Mexican culture, everyone from the children to the oldest person in the household worked and had chores to do. Everyone had a designated task depending on their age and the tasks ranged from chores around the house to milking the cows and farming. I was busier than I had ever been in my young life. I attended school like I did in the United States, but had to complete my chores around the house each day as well.

The move to Mexico, while exciting, required some adjustment. In addition to the chores, my school in Mexico was different from the one in the United States. My junior high school was in an old abandoned barn, as opposed to the modern building in the United States. We had desks and chalkboards in school, but no books, notebooks, or pens. My father often told us about walking through dirt and mud to attend school and suddenly I was doing so every day, which was new to me. As I completed junior high school, they built a better junior high school for students. If school was hard, life at home was equally challenging. My family owned farming land with chickens and roosters. We also owned cows, pigs, and horses. In the mornings before going to school, I had to feed and milk the animals. I would wake up at 5am to milk and feed the animals. After feeding the animals, I would then walk to school by 8am when classes started. Initially it would take me an hour or so to complete my chores, but with time I mastered them. The hardest part of the chores was milking the cows. Often the cows fought me and I would have to coax them before milking them. Besides the animals, I also had to work on the farm. We had to work alongside the people on the farms each day. Living in Mexico - while it was hard - was fun. We had access to the freshest fruits, vegetables, and diary. As a child growing up in Mexico, I always felt the tacos in Mexico tasted better than in the United States. I was too young to compare or understand why it tasted better. Even to this day my mouth waters at the thought of the tacos in Mexico. I now know the ingredients in the tacos made them so amazing. The ingredients were fresh, natural, and not processed in comparison to the US.

While chores and walking through dust to school made life challenging, language was a completely different challenge in itself. When I first moved to Mexico, I struggled with academic Spanish. I grew up speaking Spanish at home, but the version we spoke at home was colloquial Spanish. It was almost like I was learning Spanish again and had to adapt myself to the Spanish spoken in Mexico, as well as learning formal Spanish at school. I struggled with big words that were not used on a daily basis. With time I started getting comfortable with Spanish and I rarely conversed in English.

I was fourteen or fifteen when my parents decided to move back to the United States of America in 1993. When we moved back to Oakland, I was told I would need to repeat high school here. I started 10th grade in Oakland, California. I was assigned to Fremont High School, which was notorious for being one of the worst schools in California. Luckily, I ended up attending Skyline High School, which was in the rich side of Oakland. Skyline High School was one of the best high schools in Oakland. The high school years in America were extremely difficult on me. I couldn't transfer any of my high school credits from Mexico. I did not have any friends here. I struggled with my English, having completed most of my education in Spanish. My entire curriculum in Mexico was in Spanish. When I started high school in Oakland, I had trouble conversing in English. I would have to pause and think about the words to use to express what I wanted to. I was enrolled in ESL (English as a second language) classes in the beginning. Most of the students in my ESL classes knew little to no English. There were several people in my class who were from Mexico. We conversed in Spanish with each other, which did not help with my English speaking skills. In addition to the language, I felt academically Mexico had a higher standard of education when compared to United States. In Mexico, I had over six subjects in junior high school that we had to pass before moving on to high school. In high schools, we had ten different subjects we had to master. The school set the curriculum and everyone followed it. I found it odd that in the United States students picked their subjects and had options to skip subjects if they decided to do so. It took me more than a year and a half to get comfortable with speaking English, high school, and socializing outside my comfort zone.

I am not sure how my parents decided on moving to Oakland, but I am assuming it was because we had family there. I had family living in Hayward, Oakland, and Union City and we often gathered together during weekends and holidays. I am assuming proximity to family drove my parent's decision to move to Oakland as opposed to somewhere else in America. Oakland had a reputation of more crimes and gang related activity than anywhere else in the Bay Area. Although our neighborhood was not bad, it was not safe either. We never encountered any violence in our neighborhood, but were surrounded by neighborhoods that were gang affiliated. Our neighborhood did not give any indication of being surrounded by some of the most dangerous neighborhoods in Oakland. Kids played outside and everything seemed normal. We were often reminded of the gangs when we drove by other neighborhoods, which we had to pass through almost every day. I think my upbringing in Mexico enabled me to stay focused. I never got in trouble or associated myself with gangs.

My parents were in their mid 20's when they came to America for the first time. They have lived here for several years now, but cannot speak English fluently beyond a basic conversation. In spite of leaving Mexico for America, Mexican culture was a huge part of my childhood and upbringing. We watched Mexican television shows, my mom cooked Mexican food, and we spoke Spanish predominantly at home. In all the relocation between Mexico and America, my parents always made sure we were rooted to our culture. My dad loved having roosters as pets since he was a child. When we lived in Oakland, we owned roosters. He currently lives in San Antonio, Texas, and owns more than hundred roosters. They own lots of land in Texas where his roosters flock around. My dad never let Mexico from his heart and stayed connected to his roots. He loved farming and would always be outside working on his farm. He continues to do his bit of farming in San Antonio to this day. He owns lots of land where he puts on his farmer's hat amidst his many roosters. I think that is his happy place to this day. Family meant everything to my father and he always maintained close contacts with all our extended family, uncles, aunties, and cousins.

My father was a very influential person in my life. Since my childhood I have watched my dad work hard on his farm amidst his cows, horses, and roosters. My dedication to my work comes from my father and my upbringing. I always saw my father wake up early to work on the farm. He worked constantly and I always remember him being very busy. My father tried to instill great work ethics in us as kids. He often told us stories about people with great work ethics and how the hardworking people never wasted their lives watching television or sitting idle. "Francisco, you need to work hard if you want to succeed," he often told me as a child. His words became my mantra in life. I wanted to succeed as much as all the people whose stories my dad told me. We did not have a high school in our town. I traveled thirty-five miles to attend high school in Mexico. I traveled to the edge of the town to get a bus that would take me to the other town, where my high school was located. In spite of my high school being far, I still had to feed and milk the cows. My chores did not decrease because I had to travel further. I woke up earlier, completed my chores, and made the journey to school. I studied late at night and worked hard to get good grades. I was determined to become the man my father described in his stories. I wanted to make my dad proud of me as a person. With time I started enjoying being busy all the time. I think my tough upbringing made me who I am today. I am grateful for the parents and the life I had lived in Mexico.

I look back at my life today as a manager in a technology company in the Bay Area and I cannot help but chuckle. This was not the path I thought I would be leading in Mexico. I actually could see myself being a farmer for the rest of my life. I enjoyed working in the farm amidst the cows and horses. I think being a farm boy was in my genes and I believed I wanted to be a farmer one day. We were still in Mexico when I told my dad, "I think I have found my calling in life. I want to be a farmer for the rest of my life and I want to be a ranch owner one day." Soon after I voiced my desire to my dad, my parents told us we were moving back to the United States of America. I think the talk I had with my father played a big role in their decision to move back. I believe he wanted to expose me to a different world than our life in Mexico. When we first left Oakland for Mexico, I was a child. I did not remember much of our lives in America. I did not know of a life outside of Mexico. I still remember coming to America in 1993 as a teenager. I was amazed at the opportunities available in America. My upbringing in Mexico had formed a structure in my life. I never thought about ditching classes or getting in trouble. I was very focused and disciplined. I focused on being the man in my father's stories, even after coming to America. I never questioned the authority of my parents. They moved countries, made me adapt to different lifestyles, and I took it in my stride. Unlike the children in America, my parents never reasoned their decision with us, and we followed them without questioning their decision.

When we first moved to America with my parents, it was just my sister and I. We watched our parents work hard and build a house in Mexico before moving back to Mexico. With time our family grew with the addition of another two brothers and two sisters. Unlike my sister and I, my other siblings did not live and experience Mexico like we did. Although we are siblings, I see several differences in our personalities. They grew up in the comforts of America. They are not as hard working as I grew up to be. They are not as ambitious either and are happy in the space they are at. I have imbibed my hard working character from my life in Mexico. I am appalled when I see Mexicans portrayed as slackers and the ones doing menial jobs in the United States. Mexicans see it differently. They do not consider any job to be menial and take pride in doing the job at hand. In America, Mexicans are considered to be the ones doing the low-end jobs like janitorial services. The Mexican janitor sees that job as a source of income to feed their family. Work is part of a Mexican's DNA, regardless of what the job entitles. I see that mentality in my personality while my siblings do not see it that way. I guess I am more Mexican than they are.

When we moved to Oakland in 1993, extended family and relatives surrounded us. When I was younger, we would get together during all major holidays and other events. I loved meeting my cousins and my extended family. We looked forward to it. As my generation grew up and started families, everyone started moving farther away. With each passing year, it has become difficult to get together as a family. We manage to meet once or twice each year, but we got together more frequently before. My parents moved to San Antonio and I only get to see them once or twice a year. I miss having everyone around, meeting family more frequently, and just doing things together.

I have always wondered why my parents decided to move back to Mexico after staying in the United States for few years. I was six or seven years old and in the Mexican culture you do not question authority. I just followed my parents and walked the path with them. I always believed growing up in Mexico was a good experience for me. I was exposed to experiences other children in America could not experience. Although I had my struggles with the language there, I took it positively and made the most out of the opportunity. Each time I got comfortable with the language and culture of a place, we moved again. I never asked them but I always wondered. Today I am a father to my young son. I remember carrying him in my arms for the first time in the hospital and feeling overwhelmed. I wanted him to have the best life could offer, I wanted to make this place safe for him. I wanted him to know his culture and heritage. The answer I was searching for became clear to me as I held my son in my hands. My parents moved to America to provide better opportunities and a better life for us. When my parents moved to America, my dad worked hard and built a house in Mexico for us. When we moved back, we were living a good life in Mexico. In addition to the house, my dad owned three trucks for couple of years until we could establish our farms again. Initially we would go to Mexico during summers for couple of years to establish and oversee everything. After four years in the United States, we moved back to Mexico. When I told my dad I wanted to become a farmer, he moved us again so I could see a different world, a world where you could become anyone you wanted to, where opportunities were in abundance if you were willing to work for it. He moved us to America because he knew I could live an easier life than he did as a farmer.

My parents were born and raised in Mexico but they were not strict traditionalists. They always had an open mind, which I think helped them thrive in both cultures. They have always been open to people who were different. While my parents were hardworking, they did not have stringent rules for us to follow besides no bad words being allowed in our house. We were encouraged to communicate with each other and were free to speak our minds. They were accepting of everyone, even things they were not accustomed to. As I raise my son in America, I am appreciative of the lifestyle I was provided with while growing up. As a father, I am trying to instill the same values in my son. I want him to respect everybody and treat everyone as equals regardless of gender and race. I would want him to make good decisions, be levelheaded, and grow into someone who values hard work and family. I want him to become educated and realize the importance of education. I want him to be a good and responsible man. I won't force him into any religion, but I will expose him to different religions so he can choose when he is older. When he grows up I want to take him to Mexico so he can see where his father was born and raised. We try to expose him to the Mexican culture, food, and music as much as we can. I speak Spanish with him so he does not forget his language. We also expose him to different cultures and foods so he can be worldlier than I ever was. I was raised in a small city while he is being raised in the Bay Area. I see differences between both our childhoods, but I am still hoping to instill values that will help him make the right decisions whenever he needs to. Since my son is growing up in America, I know I cannot control him or his decisions. While I don't want to be overprotective as a father, I want to make sure he makes the right choices.

I spent my growing years in Mexico and have fond memories of my life there. I still believe we lived a better life in Mexico than in America.

In Mexico we had a big, nice house. My dad bought several acres of land and we made money by harvesting seasonal crops. We didn't have several expenses because we grew everything we needed to survive. We did not have to pay for anything besides electricity and food. With regards to food, we grew most of the produce we needed, like fruits and vegetables. Our lifestyle in Mexico did not require us to make lots of money and whatever we earned, we saved. When we moved back to Oakland, it was financially hard for us as a family. We had to pay rent and buy everything. Our apartment was a small confined space in comparison to the big farm we grew up in. I missed the open space we had in Mexico.

I have visited Mexico several times since we moved to United States. I visited Mexico five years back in 2009-2010, when my maternal grandmother passed away. Mexico was different than what I remembered from my childhood and growing years. I remember my small town was very safe when we lived there. We hardly heard of any crimes, killings, or drug related activity. Even the big cities in Mexico were safe when we lived there. Now things have changed. Mexico is no longer safe, with the drug cartels and other crime lords operating there. All my life in America, my parents talked about moving back to Mexico for retirement. Dad fostered that dream all my life. He finally realized the Mexico he left behind and the Mexico he grew up no longer exists. It is no longer safe to go back to Mexico. My parents bought a ranch in San Antonio and spend their retired life there. My dad was raised in a big family with twelve siblings. Everyone except his sister has moved to America. Most of my mom's immediate family has relocated to the larger cities in Mexico, except for one of her uncles who continues to live in our small town. We have no reason to go back to Mexico except for visiting distant relatives. I may not visit Mexico often, but I foster fond memories of my time there.

As a child I constantly shifted base between Mexico and America. While the initial days in both places were challenging because of the language barriers, I have over time felt at home in both Mexico and California. California has a big Mexican population because of the proximity to Mexico. Mexicans are often in the news because of illegal immigrants crossing the border to America. I am reminded of my roots when I hear people talk about Mexicans doing menial jobs or coming over to America illegally. I want people in America to know that Mexicans come here like the rest of the immigrants. They come to America for opportunities like everyone else in the world. I hope they stop looking down on my people because of the jobs they do. I want Americans to know that even the janitor working in their house wants to work in a professional setting. They probably could not afford to wait for that perfect opportunity to knock on their door and probably had to support a family. They work hard to provide for their family, even if their hopes and aspirations were hidden in the corners of their heart. I hope when people see a Mexican fixing their garden or doing their laundry, they would appreciate how hard they work.

I often reminisce of life I have lived. I have been fortunate to live in both Mexico and America. I have been exposed to the high-rise life as well as the simple farm boy life. I have enjoyed both equally. Whenever I see my son speak in Spanish or eat Mexican food, I think back to my life in Mexico. I cherish my upbringing in Mexico and the time I spent there. As much as I enjoyed that time of my life, I could never think about moving back to Mexico. I often wonder what would have happened had my parents stayed back in Mexico. I probably would have become a farmer, but my father decided to give me a better life. He decided to move us to America. This country has provided me with several opportunities. While I cherish every second of my life in Mexico, California is home. This is the place where I became a man, where I built my family, where I had our son. This place has given me everything I have. While Mexico holds a corner of my heart, California is and will forever be home.

I Am Moo-Hay and French Because of My English Accent!

I LOOKED OUTSIDE THE WINDOW watching snowflakes decorate the atmosphere. The entire landscape was painted white with snow. This was not my first white December, yet it never ceased to amaze me. These are small reminders of the distance I have traveled for love, the small reminders of the changes in my life that continue to intrigue and amaze me to this day. I am an immigrant in America, yet I fit right in the crowd. I walk outside my Ohio home and can blend into the ethnically diverse mix. As I celebrate my moment in the crowd, I am reminded of my uniqueness when I converse in my English accent. I always believed my name would be the least complicated aspect of my move to America being named Molly. Yet, my accent makes people call me Mow-lay, Mon-ay, Mull-lay, Mow-leen, and Moo-hay. Moo-hay happens to be my absolute favorite. I initially tried to reinforce my name, but with time I allow the person to call me whatever they intend to. I could be Mow-lay one day and Moo-hay the next. I am a white woman from Cornwall, United Kingdom, living in Ohio, America, with my thick accented British English and this is my story.

I have prayed and hoped for October 4, 2013, for the past four years and finally it arrived. I was beyond thrilled to finally make the move to America from United Kingdom. The last few days leading to October 4, 2013, I tried to soak in every little bit of my UK life. I memorized the details of the streets I had called home, but I was ready to finally live a life with my husband. It had been four years since we had lived together. Four years since I felt his warmth on my skin and seen his face in person. After years of taking solace in hearing each other's voice over the phone, I was ready to have a conversation in person. I was ready to leave behind the comforts of my phone to see the many expressions of his face as he spoke to me. This day was a journey of four years during which we compared every aspect of life in America and UK and the decision was made to make America home. We compared everything from job prospects, cost of living, and general living expenses before making the decision. When I first went back to UK, leaving my husband in 2009, we decided he was going to move to UK. I had a good job in UK and he could find a job there. As we were preparing for his British visa, circumstances changed. My husband got laid off from his job and was able to find another one quickly. In the process, he realized it would be easier for me to find a job in the US than it would be for him to get a job in UK. So the decision was made and US would become the place we would eventually settle in. After the decision was made, the endless barrage of paperwork leading to my visa and interviews began. There were moments filled with nervousness, doubts, and endless waits which culminated to this day October 4, 2013. I boarded the flight and arrived in Ohio in 2013. The flight ride was long, and the restlessness I felt waiting to see his face made the ride longer than the hours expected. I walked out of the airport and saw him stand in front of me. I was overcome with emotions as I ran to hold him in my arms. We were finally together, and all the apprehensions I felt leaving my life behind were validated in that second. I could not wait to begin our life together finally.

I looked outside as our car made its way to our home in Ohio. I had moved around United Kingdom until I settled in Cornwall, United Kingdom. Cornwall was in the Southwest of England and was home. I worked as a schoolteacher in UK before I decided to follow love to

America. I am not sure how big Cornwall was, but it felt more spacious, free, and larger in comparison to London. Cornwall was less crowded in comparison to London with its palaces and gardens, but Cornwall was special. Southwest England was filled with abbeys and castles enriched by dark fairytales and folktales. While Cornwall has the European castles and palaces, it also had villages and countryside reminiscent of the simple European life. The water around Cornwall provided the much needed island feel with its warm air. As our car drove down the street, I instantly missed the water and warmth of Cornwall. I knew moving to America would take some adjustment, but everyday life seemed to be the greatest adjustment for the Brit in me. The first few days were spent listening to my American husband as he gave me a crash course on all things America. I grew up using washers and dryers, but the first time I had to do laundry I was perplexed. They did not look anything like the washers and dryers back home. The doors on the washer and dryers locked different in comparison to the appliances back in UK. My husband gave me a crash course on how to use a washer and dryer. It felt like I was from a different planet and was being introduced to the concept of washer and dryer. Every time I got in a car and had to sit on the right, I felt like the driver. It made me nervous being a non-driver. It took me several months before I got used to driving on the other side of the street.

Ohio, America, is different from Cornwall, UK. Beyond the architecture, wildlife and landscape being different, Ohio is cheaper in comparison to UK. Rent and gas are way cheaper than UK and there are several social entertainment options available at acheaper price. However, health care is not free in the US, which balances out everything else being cheap here. UK is more progressive than Ohio in its acceptance of different people and lifestyle choices. While US is accepting to people, I think UK is more forward thinking than Ohio. I realized British were a rare species in Ohio. The funniest thing about being British in Ohio includes the many times someone thought I was French from my accent. I am surprised when people ask me if I know their friend or relative in UK because I am from there. I am not sure if they think UK has five people or where that concept comes from, but it always gives me a good chuckle when I am asked that question. When I first arrived in Ohio, I was eager to learn about the place I was going to call my home. I did what I was expected to do. I Googled Ohio and grazed upon some interesting and whacky Ohio facts, which got me thinking about the place. It is illegal in the state of Ohio to get a fish drunk. While it might make fishing easy, I wondered how someone could get a fish drunk for starters. Ohio, specifically Dresden, is home to world's largest apple holding basket. In Paulding, Ohio, a policeman could bite a dog to silence it. I am not sure how that could silence a dog, but it would be amusing to watch who might win the battle. These interesting facts made me excited about living in Ohio.

I have visited America before I decided to move here permanently and did not imagine much of a culture shock. Britain and America share a common link in different facets such as language, food, music, and TV, so I thought I knew America. I expected the transition to be easy in comparison to if I had moved to China or elsewhere. I was surprised when I was perplexed while using the washer and dryer. After being perplexed for a few days, I decided to gradually immerse myself in American culture. I decided to walk to get my morning coffee similar to my routine in UK. I wanted to keep it as normal as I could. The streets were different, the country was different, but my routine stayed regular. As I walked for my morning coffee, I started understanding my surroundings; the streets started feeling familiar.

I had been in America for three weeks. I had started using household appliances such as the washer, dryer, and cookers with much ease. I had begun getting used to random people greeting me at stores with a, "Hi, how are you?" Initially I felt weird, but I had begun enjoying it. I was ecstatic to receive a new American phone number and was gearing up to text my family in UK. I signed up for a phone plan and ensured they supported international calling. I paid my fee and was ready to call my family when I realized not only did it not have an international plan, but also did not support Blackberry's. I could not call, text, or even check my emails on my phone. I had no connection with my family in UK. I had always been in touch with them. I felt homesick and could not function. My surroundings were new, my hubby and I were apart for four years so we were going through our adjustment phase, and in everything that was new my family back home was my constant solace. Not being able to contact them made me sad. My husband came to my rescue, and helped me talk through the sadness I was feeling. We signed up for a new plan and I was able to talk to my family again.

My husband and I lived our entire lives miles apart, and that adds the necessary cultural humor in our lives. Like most people I assumed the move from Britain to America would not be too challenging, but English has been the greatest challenge of them all. We both speak English, but US English and British English are worlds apart. When I moved to Ohio, I was completely surprised by the tornado-warning siren. Initially it was extremely nerve racking, especially as areas around were hit badly. We had heavy gusts of wind with lightning, thunder, and flickering power. On one such dark night, my husband was confused when I told him I had to use a torch to find my way. My husband expected to see me carrying a flaming stick, which in America was a torch. What we English call torch was flashlight in America. My husband thought I was rather odd.

There are several aspects of UK I miss terribly, my family, friends, and the food. I have realized food in America is very processed with hormones, chemicals, and other additives. Food back in UK was very fresh. I had heard about Twinkies before I could come to US through the movie Ghostbusters in 1984. My husband was eager to introduce me to the American legend "Twinkie". Twinkie is a sponge finger filled with cream filling. I was ready for my Twinkie experience. I expected it to be more on the lines of jam filled Swiss rolls in UK, but the Twinkie sponge was denser in comparison. The cream filling felt very processed and wasn't my favorite. Needless, my husband was happy to finish the rest of the Twinkie's for me. Corn dogs, another American staple, were my next conquest. I was looking forward to trying a corn dog after all the ravings from my husband and the people around. Corn dog is a hot dog dipped in corn flour batter and fried. While the hot dog tasted like every other hot dog I have tasted, the batter was too oily and strong for my liking. America has a strange fixation with peanut butter and jelly. I had heard about peanut butter and jelly long before I moved to America. I was more than happy to share my husband's peanut butter fixation until I tasted my first peanut butter and jelly sandwich. My husband loves his peanut butter and I let him enjoy that aspect of the American life. I am not a peanut butter fan. I am surprised to see peanut butter stuffed pizza crust when I walk down the store aisle. Peanut butter is too American for this British girl!

I am a white, red-haired British girl with a thick English accent. Being a natural redhead, I have always stood out in the crowd, yet when I talk I have always blended in. The hardest part about the move to America, besides the actual visa process and the subtle cultural differences, has been my accent. Often people find it very hard to understand my accent. It does not help being the only British person I have ever encountered in Ohio. I feel like an endangered species or worse an alien from a different planet every time I speak. Something as simple as my name Molly sounds like Mow-ly when said with an English accent to Americans. Alphabets of the English language challenge me too. In British

English the letter Z is pronounced as Zed as opposed to Zee in America. It took some thought to initially break free from the zed, but now I can say zee without thinking about it. The grocery stores and restaurants have too many choices when compared to UK. Initially I felt I was taking too much time to order food or pick up different foods. I have lived in London all my life and have never driven myself anywhere. The public transportation was very good in London, making it easy to get from point A to B. In Ohio, the public transportation is really bad. I find the roads in Ohio are very bad in comparison to the roads in London. The fact that I am restricted because I cannot drive really annoys me.

One of the things I love about being an expat is receiving packages from back home. I love receiving parcels and letters from friends and family. As a child I loved writing letters. The advent of computers somehow replaced the love I had for writing. I developed my love for writing letters again after I moved to America. Every time I received a parcel or letter from UK, it reminds me of home. It takes me back in time to my days with friends and family. As I sit with my cup of tea opening my parcels or reading my letters, I find myself falling in love with the art of letter writing again. I used to work as a schoolteacher before I could move to America. I started blogging and have a blog called "themovetoamerica.wordpress.com" which chronicles my journey to America. I started my blog while in UK to document the visa process and the emotional turmoil associated with it. I started blogging so I can offer a realistic view on what it takes to move to a new country. I wanted to provide a realistic view of America. Today, my blog is a gateway to stay in touch with my family and friends back home. I continue to blog about my experiences in America, and hope my blog is helping others make the transition easily.

I have been living in America since 2013, and often reflect on my life here. There have been some losses and several gains. I have been able to live a life with my husband, which seemed out of reach in United Kingdom. I have realized some of the things I call losses are not forever losses, just out of reach. Recently, America banned British chocolate brand Cadbury in the United States. I have tried Hershey's and honestly I think American chocolates are inferior in quality to British chocolate. I am not sure if I would have felt the sense of loss I felt reading the news. I pondered why they would ban something so amazing. As an expat in a foreign country, loss of identity and self is something every person who has moved from familiar to foreign deals with. It is small in comparison, but for someone like me that bite of chocolate reminds me of home, familiarity, and the life I left behind.

Moving to America has been a blessing in disguise. I moved to America following love and hoping to build a life together. In return I have learned more about myself as a person. I have always been shy and my shyness has prevented me from doing certain things in UK. Since moving to America, I have realized I have had to find innovative ways to combat my shyness as I maneuver out of my comfort zone. I have often felt like a fish out of water being a foreigner in America. I have moved to America and made a home in the corners of Ohio with my husband. Yet, there is a part of me that misses the familiarity of United Kingdom. I always knew I would miss my friends and family with this move. I am amazed at how much I miss the simpler aspects of UK I took for granted. I miss the good cream tea. I miss the sputtering rain of United Kingdom and often feel pangs of jealousy as my family and friends update social media with rain updates. Ohio gives me days of sunshine and snow in two consecutive days, and in some ways I miss the expected days of rain. I am tired of the surprise weather conditions of Ohio. There are several things I miss about United Kingdom. I feel at home in Ohio, but it is still very new. I might feel at ease in Ohio, but my home continues to be the country I have known all my life. United Kingdom is the place where my family and friends reside in, where the streets are familiar, and the place that holds the strings to my heart. United Kingdom is the place of my birth and it is home. Ohio is the place where I live and have built a life in. Ohio is also the place I share with my husband. It is also home because he makes me feel at home in Ohio. (PS: For more on Molly's journey and experiences, follow her at themovetoamerica.wordpress.com)

One Inch from Heaven & a Quarter Inch from Hell!

I WALKED OUTSIDE NEW YORK airport and felt the cold breeze engulf me in seconds. It was 20 degrees outside and I was dressed in summer attire. I was not prepared for the cold New York weather. I rushed back into the airport. The security guard at the airport saw me rush back in and asked if I was okay. I told him I was okay, but needed some coverage from the cold breeze. That was my first tryst with America, and for this African boy from Sierra Leone, the snowflakes in the air and cold wind reminded me of the miles I have traveled from Sierra Leone.

Sierra Leone, an Anglo form country in the west coast of Africa, is my home. I have lived there from the moment I came into this world and I expected to live there for the rest of my life until the civil war in Sierra Leone broke out in 1991. The political conflict lasted for ten to eleven years during which there were killings, unrest and uncertainty. I can never forget that day the world around me changed in a second. Before the war I never thought about leaving Sierra Leone, but after the war erupted I was forced to leave. I did not have a strategy on how I wanted to relocate. I was focused on leaving my country and if it required walking to safety, then that was my goal. I first moved to the main city hoping to complete my education. When the war spread to the main city, I traveled to Guinea, whose capital is Conakry. Guinea Conakry was French. I stayed there for a month, but soon after the war spilled over which prompted me to move yet again. I moved to Senegal hoping this would be it. As soon as I landed in Senegal, I realized people did not speak English. I stayed there for a short span and eventually moved to Guinea Bissau. When I reached the border of Guinea Bissau, the guards asked me if I spoke Creole. I said yes. I thought Creole is a broken language of an official language. I learned soon enough I was wrong. I received a permit to enter the country. I thought Creole was Patwa (Jamaican Creole which is English based Creole language), but in Guinea Bissau people spoke Portuguese. I was in Guinea Bissau for a total of eight hours before I knew I had to leave. I traveled back to Senegal and was received with hostility by the French. I looked at the map and decided to follow the path to Gambia. Gambia seemed like the right country for me. They spoke English like Sierra Leone and welcomed me with open arms. I stayed there for a year and tried to get my life back on track. By then the war had spread to Sierra Leone, Liberia, and some of the neighboring countries.

Gambia opened a world of opportunities and I was determined to take advantage of it. I decided to continue my education, but faced challenges which made it difficult. I got a part time job to help pay for my tuitions. During that time, I decided to write an international examination to obtain visas to other countries. I decided to write the exam for United Kingdom and United States of America. I got excellent grades and had the option to pursue education in UK or USA. I used the certificate from my school and the international exam scores to apply for visa to both these countries. A month and half later I received an interview call from the United States Embassy. I was issued a visa to USA and three weeks later I received an interview call from the UK embassy. I declined the UK interview and decided to come to America. When I arrived in Gambia, I met people from Liberia who spoke English. We became friends over time. We lived in the same neighborhood and often interacted with each other. They were fortunate to travel to America before I did and we maintained our friendship in spite of the distance. I received my visa to attend college in Georgia. This was soon after 9/11 and everything had changed. All colleges required a big down payment of about $5000 to $7000. I did not have that kind of money on me. I decided not to attend college in Georgia. Instead I decided to fly to New York City where my friends were located.

I stood at the New York airport waiting for my friends to pick me up. I expected my friends to be waiting at the airport for me. I peeked through the airport glass trying to catch a glimpse of them. I looked for them and did not have a cell phone on me to call them. They were driving around the airport in their car. I had never seen them drive a car back home. Eventually we found each other and they drove me to New Jersey from New York. They lived in a small apartment and had no place for me. I stayed on their couch with a blanket for a month. The first month in America was extremely challenging. I came here on a student visa, but did not have the financial means to afford college. I did not drive or own a car. I could not travel around. I was sleeping in my friend's living room. The highlight of my day included hanging out with my friend for the few minutes he came home. I hardly saw him otherwise. It was after 9/11 and the international student visa rules were stringent. I was paranoid I would be hunted in America. I called Fort Valley State University and explained my situation to them. They asked me to report myself to the immigration authorities. While living on the couch, I contacted some of my school friends in California. They asked me to check for asylum or refugee status in San Francisco. I contacted immigration and they invited me to their office. I packed my bags and moved to California.

Besides inviting me to the immigration office, they sent me the website where I could find the forms to apply. As I looked at the legal documents and procedure ahead of me, I was convinced I would need an immigration attorney. When I did my research I found out they charged

$5000-$7000 for representation. As much as I was in dire need of their services, I could not afford them. I was living in my friend's apartment. I could have asked someone for the money, but I have always been independent. I never asked my friends to take me places, so asking for money was farfetched. The attorney offered to help me through the process, but I was expected to pay him $5000 when I started working. My friends assured me it was the right thing to do. So I got into a verbal agreement with the attorney and did not get anything signed on paper stating the above. When immigration called me for the interview, my attorney did not show up. I lost possibly my only opportunity and the thought made me nervous. I went to Hayward in California to meet him in person. I told him my next interview was next week. He looked at his calendar for few minutes. "I have a conflict on my calendar and cannot make it to the appointment next week," were his exact words to me. I was stumped, but I knew I would have to walk this path alone. I completed all my paperwork and he signed the document saying if there were any issues, he would represent me. He was my insurance policy in case I got deported.

The day of my interview arrived as I collected every paper during my stay in America. I had everything in my backpack as I walked into the interview. I had evidence of everything from pictures of the bodily scar I got during the rush, pictures, and visa. As I walked into the interview room, I was scared. When I decided to move to America, I did it for security and to help my family back home. I was scared I would be deported back to Sierra Leone. Some of the questions thrown at me during the interview baffled me. Describe the first thing you see when you walk out of your house, the interviewer asked me. The questions ranged from personal, to questions on infrastructure, and vegetation of my surroundings. I learned from research if you did not cite a school in the neighborhood, or a park, the immigration authorities could flag you for a personal visit and would likely put you on the deportation list.

Fortunately, I was granted asylum after the interview.

While being approved for asylum was exciting and validating, the roadblocks along the way were many. In addition to the situation with the lawyer, my friends I was living with also turned against me. While I was going through my immigration problems with the lawyer, my friend suggested I get married to someone he knew who was a citizen. I told him I wasn't ready for a relationship and did not want to go down that route. I wanted to try for asylum before getting married. I was not emotionally or financially ready to be married. I told him if my partner was the sole breadwinner and I could not support her, I don't think the marriage would work. I guess my friend took the rejection personal. While I was waiting for my asylum to be approved, I set up my mails so my friends could call me at my work if I received anything from Immigration. Immigration sent a letter for my biometrics fingerprinting appointment to my home address, which my friend received but did not give it to me. I never saw that letter from immigration. A few weeks later I received mail from immigration saying I was in trouble. I knew it looked bad. I had come to America as a student, ended up not going to college, and now missed the biometric appointment. I went to the immigration office the next day and they gave me two options. They would send me another letter with the biometrics appointment date and if I missed that one I would be on the deportation list. When I confronted my friend, he said he never received it. I went to the post office and they confirmed they had delivered that specific mail. I had to reapply again and it delayed the process by six to eight months. My work permit expired by the end of the process. I received all the papers the second time because I changed my mailing address to my office. I was really upset, but did not confront him regarding the issue. I just wanted to move on.

When I reached America, my only goal was to complete my education and succeed in life. Initially I had to make the hard decision to not attend Fort Valley State University, but I continued to pursue that dream. I applied to some colleges and was classified as a foreign student everywhere because my asylum was not granted yet. I did not want to take too many loans and be in debt. I had several things working against me in America. Firstly I was black and secondly I was African in America. I had to be realistic in deciding how marketable I was if I pursued certain degrees or courses. I weighed my options in deciding the path I was comfortable with personally and financially.

Even before I could reach America, I had a very realistic view of the place because of the people I encountered in my life. When I was in Sierra Leone, I had friends from all over the world, including America. They were part of the International Christian Youth Exchange program and some of them were part of the Peace Corps, as well. They came to our schools and colleges and interacted with us. We exchanged cultural information, such as life in America, lifestyle, freedom, the differences, and how people lived their lives here. Besides that, I had friends in Germany and other Western countries who briefed me on the life there. I was prepared to do whatever it took to succeed in America and I knew the path would not be easy.

All my life I have fostered a dream to become a farmer like my daddy. As a kid growing up in Sierra Leone, I accompanied my daddy to our farm and watched him be a farmer. My daddy is a farmer who does subsistence farming and shifting cultivation. I inherited my dreams of commercial farming from him. When the consulate asked me what I wanted to study in America, I said I wanted to learn new technologies related to farming and cultivation that I could implement back in my country. I believed agriculture could improve an economy. I always noticed people in my country owned land and refused to share it. If two people owned land back home and had to allow the other person walk their land to get to their land, they would refuse, thus preventing the other person from cultivating. This kind of selfishness has made African economy not thrive. I hoped with my education and new technologies I could change Sierra Leone for the better. However, I ended up not doing anything with farming and technology in America. I started working with special needs children. I always remembered people telling me I need to be open to survive in the western world. My friend who worked in this facility asked me to come by if I wanted to work there and he could hook me up with a job. I hauled myself to the facility and ended up working with special needs children. It was very different from the life I envisioned for myself in Africa, but I knew I had no support system here. Back home, I could have gone back to my family for financial support. I did not want to be dependent on any of my friends, and this job helped me become independent.

My life in Sierra Leone was different than in America. We used to take a basket and walk the distance to the market for our shopping. Back then, they did not give us shopping bags, but now you can buy a shopping bag for ten cents. Our markets were similar to the farmers markets here and they sold everything there. We also can find mini stores owned by individuals from Guinea Conakry. When I first reached America, I was really glad they had pictures with all their foods. I would look at the picture and figure out the dish had bread and meat before ordering. Initially I did not go out to eat. I did not own a car and biking far distances can be tiring. My asylum was yet to be approved and I was scared I would get in trouble. I did not want to be deported, so I stayed inside.

Sierra Leone is an Anglo based country where English is the spoken language. Yet, I did not expect the challenges with communication I encountered here in America. I think there is a difference between knowing a language and having an accent. Very often when I speak in my accented English, people assume I cannot speak English. On one such instance, I was taking a bus to Hayward to meet my attorney. A Caucasian guy who seemed lost was looking for directions. I was standing at the bus stop along with another couple and students from the nearby college. The Caucasian guy walked around asking for directions. Some of the students had their headphones on, while some others were reading their book. When I noticed no one was paying attention, I tried to help him with directions. He completely ignored me because of my accent and walked away. I could not believe he would ignore the help I was offering. A couple who was standing behind me watched this whole scenario unfold. We boarded the same bus and we started conversing. They asked me where my accent was from. When I said Africa, they asked me the specific country I was from. I told them, "Thank you! Most people think Africa is a country." We exchanged numbers and continued to stay in touch.

I have lived in America for over nine years now. Along the way I have encountered several challenges, ranging from communication to racism. I never acknowledge racism because I believe these things exist in an all-black country like Sierra Leone, too. At my work, people use my articulation as an excuse for not understanding what I say, even after working together for three-four years. I tell them we can always email each other in order to avoid miscommunication. I have a typical African name which has been a source of discrimination as well. When I apply for a new job, the first thing they see is my name, Benedict. I am marginalized instantly. I conducted a social experiment, if I can call it that. My friend with a Caucasian name who worked in Marines applied to a job that I had applied to. He had no skills for the job, while I was working in the field. Yet, he was called for an interview and had to decline. Although I have a very African name, I have noticed Caucasians try to pronounce my name correctly. They make an effort to learn it. Some of the other ethnicities cannot pronounce my name, so I have shortened it to Ben. Although I prefer being called Benedict, Ben is the shortened

American version of my name.

Being African in America is a challenge in itself. I had often heard that African Americans are different from Africans. While that might be true, I always believed we all originated from the same continent Africa. I never fed into the misconception until I started living in America and experienced it. At one of my jobs, an African American man who was in his 50's or 60's worked closely with me. During one of our conversations he told me, "You guys are lucky. You guys came here on your own will. Our forefathers came here in chains." That statement surprised me as I wondered how I was responsible for that happening. Genetically we might share the same forefathers if we trace the ancestry. While some African Americans make an effort to find their roots in Africa, most people are content being called African American. Europeans take pride in being called Italian American, or Austrian American, but African Americans are happy being under the bucket called African American. You never see them proudly say I am a Sierra Leone American or Nigerian American if they are born here. Africa is not a country, but a continent. African Americans have the technology and financial resources to trace their roots if they want to. As an African in America, I feel they want to be on the superior side. They'd rather be American than African. They have very little knowledge about Africa and it comes from whatever media feeds them, which is far from the truth. The old African American man was weird. Some days he would talk directly to me while on other days he would use the radio to communicate with me. He would mimic how Africans talked and make fun of us. He would sometimes try to test my loyalty to my country and continent. I patiently endured it all until he began testing my loyalty to Africa. I told him, "Look, there is nothing you can do or say that would make me change how I feel about Africa." It bothered me a lot sometimes because I am from Sierra Leone, Africa. Until they start accepting their roots, the divide between Africa and African Americans will forever exist.

I have traveled a long way from home to where I am today. I came here alone without my family. When the war erupted in Sierra Leone, I was staying in a different city than where my family was located. I could not say good bye to my parents and siblings. I left my country with a hope they were safe. Mobile phones were very expensive, so we used our landline more. When the war suddenly erupted, everyone was dispersed so we could not converge for even a goodbye. I am the second oldest in my family. When I left my country I did not know where I would end up. All I was looking for was some security and peace of mind. I wanted security for my family and myself. They sent me to school hoping I could become independent and help them in whatever way possible. I had that responsibility at the back of my head as I made that journey from home. It's been nine years since I reached America. I have since then established a life in California. I got married to a wonderful woman who I met at work. We became friends along the way and decided to get married. She is from Sierra Leone, too, and I think our combined experiences brought us together. It fascinates me that I married a Sierra Leone in America when my first girlfriend back home in Sierra Leone was an American Caucasian girl.

My wife and I got married in America in front of some of her family. My parents and siblings could not attend my wedding. It bothered my wife that my parents could not attend our wedding. In order to ease her burdens, I cultivated parents in America. I guess cultivated is not the right word, or should I say I adopted a parent. He came for our wedding. We had a traditional wedding in America. We have three boys together now, and I always struggle with teaching them their roots. We speak in our language with our kids, but they turn around and tell us, "Daddy, why are you talking in Spanish?" I tell them, "It is not Spanish." I try to explain my culture to them. I am not trying to force it down their throats. I want to introduce my culture and my life before I came to America. They see African children on the television and they call them "African people". When we look at the world geography books and they see Africa, they say African people. I tell them your mom and dad are from Africa, too. They are young, but eventually I am hoping they will accept their African roots.

Every time I see how Africa is portrayed in American media, it really bothers me. When the war broke out in Sierra Leone, we saw several organizations take advantage of the plight of people there. They take horrible pictures of the poverty there and publicize it in the media saying this is how Africa is like. People who have lived in Africa know there are two sides to the coin, just like in America or anywhere else in the world. There is poverty and there is richness, too. They use those images to collect as little as a dollar. When two million people give a dollar, they make two million dollars. They use that money, which is tax exempt, to build big mansions. If they use that money on the homeless people in America, they could eliminate some of the homelessness around here. When I lived in my country, I did not think there was poverty in America, which is why they were taking those horrible pictures. When I came here, I was shocked to see homeless Americans, too. Back home, we never thought America even had potholes, let alone poverty or homelessness.

The portrayal of Africans and Africa in America really bothered me initially. It bothered me in spite of having a realistic view of America. My friends and acquaintances back home always told me what to expect in America. I remember when I was in Gambia, I met this Caucasian guy who helped me create my first email address. During our conversation, he gave me a very realistic view of what life was like in America. I remember him asking for my first and last name for the email. As I was giving him the information, he said I will create it as Benedict whatever. To this day my email still says Benedict whatever. People back home think America is an inch away from heaven. After living here, I think it is a quarter inch from hell. No one cares about you. It is all about self, power, and money.

I have fond memories of my life in Sierra Leone before the war erupted. Life was simple and normal. People went about minding their own business. We did not have public transportation and trains in Sierra Leone. We had some helicopters, but that was reserved for the rich people. We rode our bikes everywhere, which included going to play soccer. Here everything is congested. You have no time for anything, which causes stress. It was very relaxing back home. You went to work or school for eight hours and could go back home. People were happier to do their eight hours, go home, and spend time with their family. Of course, there is eminent corruption back in Sierra Leone at the expense of poor people. There is corruption here, too, but people are held accountable for things here. I always believe freedom of speech in America comes with a price. Speaking your mind can get you in trouble here. Back home, you can speak your mind with no repercussions. I remember I could walk outside my house at 3am without worrying about being mugged or robbed at gunpoint. The only things we had to worry about were snakes and getting bit by them. It has changed since the war erupted, but I spent all my childhood not being afraid of getting robbed or killed. I miss having that freedom here.

There is an abundance of everything in America. It is extremely difficult to make the right choice with that kind of abundance and availability. There is an abundance of opportunities to choose a criminal path here. I work with people who are dealing with disabilities, which I attribute to lack of family support here. Loneliness is a constant here. In Sierra Leone, we have people who are traumatized and don't have resources like America does. However, we do not have arms on the street and they call their family for support.

I have been in America for nine years now and I often think back to the journey I have traveled. I remember the day the war erupted in Sierra Leone like it was yesterday. I endured the war and hoped it was resolved every morning. I hoped with each dawn that life would return back to normal, but it did not. I had to make the hard decision to leave behind family and friends in search of security. I was looking for security and peace of mind, which I found in America. When I think about home, I think about Sierra Leone. I miss my family and friends. That is home. We might do things archaic, but I like the simplicity. Biologically that is where I belong and that is home. But America has also become home for me. I am indebted to America because she accepted me when I had nowhere to go and for whom I am. She is my adopted mother and will always own me. As much as America owns me, I am aware that if I make a mistake, they can take my papers away and kick me back to Sierra Leone. Sierra Leone is my security blanket and will always forgive me for my mistakes because I grew up there. I would never have left Sierra Leone had the war not erupted. She makes me nostalgic and takes me back in time to a place when life was simple.

Is it For Here or to Go?

I AM ONE AMONG THE MANY Filipinos in America. While walking down the street, I could blend into the crowd. I could pass off as someone who was born in America. Yet, when I speak I connect back to Philippines with my accent. My accent lets people know I am a foreigner in America. Even after living in the United States of America for twenty-four years, Philippines continues to be my identity. I was born and raised in Luzon in Philippines until May 30, 1991, when I first moved to the United States of America as an electrical engineer. Before May 1991, I belonged to Philippines. Luzon in Philippines is 250 miles north of Manila. Luzon is the main island of Philippines. The country has three big islands namely Luzon, Visaya and Mindanao, and as many as 7,105 smaller islands. Luzon is the business center of Philippines. It is the biggest and most important economic islands of Philippines. My childhood was spent in Luzon, Philippines, breathing the tropical, humid island air, living the simple life, and splurging on fruits such as mangoes and bananas. Until America beckoned me on May 30, 1991, I had called Philippines my home.

My earliest memories of my life in the Philippines include playing on our family farm where I spent most of my free time. My family made its livelihood from planting rice, vegetables, tobacco, and fishing. There are two major seasons in the Philippines -namely the wet and dry season. The wet season runs from June through November and the dry season runs from December through March. During the rainy season, rice was cultivated. The dry season was ideal for the cultivation of tobacco, vegetables, and tropical fruits such as mangoes, pineapples, bananas, avocadoes, rambutans, and durians. We have an unlimited yearlong supply of coconuts, too. Besides farming, we also raised chickens, goats, and pigs in our backyard. My life in Philippines was very simple and stress free. I was educated in a Catholic school from elementary through high school. The Jesuit priests who came to the Philippines in 1581 ran my school. They built schools and colleges all around the country. 85% of the Philippines followed Christianity, making it the fifth largest Christian country in the world.

When I was sixteen years old, my family moved to Manila. My brother and sister finished their college in Manila when I started my college. I received my Bachelor's degree in electrical engineering in Manila and started working for an engineering and construction company. I traveled to different parts within the country building Power Substations and Transmission lines. Initially it was exciting, but with time I got tired of my assignment. At this juncture, I interviewed and received an offer at another engineering consulting company in Manila. Manila, like most big cities, was bustling with nightlife. I was single when I lived in Manila and enjoyed myself. I partied every night with my friends or went out to enjoy the nightlife. I was care free as a single man in Manila and enjoyed every party scene available to us. In 1985, I got married to my beautiful wife and settled down into a family life. I landed a job in Saudi Arabia the year I got married and decided to pursue that opportunity. I lived in the Middle East, particularly Saudi Arabia and Bahrain, for three years after which I moved back to the Philippines to work for an American company. I worked at that branch for a while after which I was assigned to Guam, which was an US Territory. I led projects all over the island of Micronesia. During this time, my petition to immigrate to America was approved. On May 30, 1991, I arrived in the United States of America.

It was 8pm on a cold May evening when I first set foot outside San Francisco airport. The cold air washed through my body making me freeze. The weather was different than the warm tropical air in Philippines that welcomed visitors when they stepped outside the airport. It was 8pm, yet it felt like 5pm. The sun was still out and the sky was bright with daylight. I found it very odd that it was so bright at night. I was excited to be in America, but I missed my family back in the Philippines, which made me very lonely. The move to America was a calculated one. I knew my sister who lived in America had filed a petition with Immigration so I could move to America. I knew it was a matter of time before I moved here. I was prepared to live in America. Yet, when I moved here I felt extremely lonely. I felt a gamut of conflicting emotions when I moved to the United States of America. While I was excited, I was extremely sad to leave my family behind. Initially, I moved alone to America, leaving my wife and two young children in the Philippines. I did not know when I would be reunited with them, which made the journey excruciatingly hard. While uncertainty of living together stared us in the face, I was hoping this move could open opportunities for my children.

When I first landed in America, I was amazed at how colorful everything was. I imagined America to be colorful with their color televisions and diversity of the people. I was used to the black and white television in Philippines. When I first turned on the television in America, I was convinced of my image of America. During my first week in America, I decided to get food from McDonald's. At the counter they asked me what I would like to order. The lady spoke too fast for me to understand and when I asked them to repeat themselves, they could not understand my accent. It took us few tries before we could get the order. I felt accomplished, but my bubble burst right after when they asked me if it was "for here" or "to go". I had no idea what those words meant. In the

Philippines we used "bring home" for to go. Initially American English and slangs were extremely challenging. People in America spoke English too fast, which made it hard to understand. This one time at work we had a supplier who was presenting his products to us. As he was explaining his products, I could not understand what he was saying. I made him repeat multiple times until I was in sync with him and could answer his queries. This happened several times at work. Initially when I started working in America, my coworkers would make fun of my accent. My Caucasian coworkers would tease my pronunciation initially, but with time they stopped teasing me. I am assuming they got used to the accent with time.

My wife and I had a long distance marriage for the first year I was in the United States of America. I called them twice a week over the phone to talk to them. I was concerned how she was managing alone in Philippines. We had family back home, which made it easier than if she was in a place with no support system. We had two young children who were attending preschool in Philippines. It was very difficult for me. I was in a foreign country by myself while my family was back at home. When I returned home from work, the loneliness of an empty house was unnerving. I was used to the chaos of the kids around the house, and the loneliness really bothered me. I don't think I ever got used to the silence around the house. Living alone and being away from family was the loneliest feeling I ever experienced in my life. I kept telling myself I was making this sacrifice for my children. Luckily, a year after I arrived in America my family joined me here. I was excited to finally have them with me. I made the move to America for my children. I wanted to give them opportunities I did not have as a child. I was excited for them to live the life I envisioned for them.

The initial days when my family moved to America were extremely difficult. Our life back in the Philippines was comfortable. We worked five days a week and had the weekends to ourselves. During the weekends we went out to the beach, or movies, or to the park for a picnic. Either way, weekends were family days. My wife worked as well, but we had help around the house to take care of things. For long holidays such as Christmas, we traveled outside the city or back to our village to meet our family. My wife was working in Philippines, but she had to find a job here. We uprooted our lives in Philippines. I found the process of starting over in America challenging. I spent the first year living with my sister and her family. When my family moved here after a few months, I decided to find a place for ourselves so we could have our privacy and give my sister her privacy. We always had a support system and help back in Philippines while raising our kids. Initially life was very scary in America as we tried to adjust to the new surroundings. Everything was new for my family, and it took them a while to adjust to the American way of life. My kids attended private preschools in Philippines. While they were fluent in English, they had some challenges adjusting to the American accent. Since they were young, they adjusted to the American ways easily.

In between surviving the new culture and building a home here, we went from a family of four to a family of five. Raising children in a new culture added its own challenges for us. My wife and I were raised in the Philippines and our culture was a big part of who we were. We spoke in our language at home and ensured we followed Filipino cultures and traditions. Although our kids replied in English when spoken to in our language, we are assured they understand our language. During family gatherings we talked about our life back in Philippines so they are aware of their culture. We cook Filipino food at home. My youngest son was born in America while his siblings were born in Philippines. He has learned our culture through the eyes of his siblings, which always makes me proud. I see several differences between how I was raised in Philippines to how my children are being raised here. Here in the United States, children are not intimidated by anything because of the freedom. When I was growing up, my parents were very strict. In addition to parents being strict in disciplining us, close relatives and teachers helped with ensuring the kids were being raised with good manners. Here, everything falls upon the parent, which is very intimidating. Today when I look back on how I raised my children, I am clueless. When I watch my kids now I know I survived the process. Two of my children are grown up and on their own. My youngest will start college this year. As a parent I am proud of my children and the way they have embraced our culture. It is important for my wife and I that our children know about Philippines.

I came to America on May 30, 1991. As I look back on our life for the past twenty-four years, I see a new America in comparison. When I came here in 1991, it was the beginning of technology boom and there was an abundance of jobs. If you were in the technology field, you could find a job in days. Gas was $0.85 a gallon and groceries were very cheap. Today, it is hard to find a part time job. When my kids were in high school, I remember they had a hard time finding a part time job. Good, decent paying jobs are hard to find these days. In addition to the lack of jobs, everything is very expensive. The only way to guarantee a decent life is to have a college degree. This puts you over the curve and gives you an edge while looking for a job.

I have lived in America for twenty-four years now. I should be used to the isolated lifestyle in America, but I am not. Life in America is very different when compared to the Philippines. In America, life is mechanical and routine. My life revolves around going to work, going back home, and starting the whole process again. I don't have relatives and extended family to support me when I have problems. I am on my own for the most part. I have my family here with me and they are my only solace.

In spite of not having the support system, America has enabled me to see my children grow. Back in the Philippines after college, people go abroad and away from family for work. I could have been away from home had I not made the decision to move to America. America helped me see my children grow into adults, which I am very indebted for.

I remember the moment I boarded the flight to America, bidding adieu to my wife and young children like it was yesterday. My children were six and seven years old then. The years have passed since that day, yet every detail is engraved in my memory. I see the passage of time when I see my children visit me. Today they are in their thirties. I see time that has passed by when I see them. They remind me of the twenty-four years I have lived in America. They remind of the twenty-four years that have passed since I visited Philippines. In these twenty-four years I have yearned to visit my family and friends back in Philippines. When I think about Philippines, I am reminded of my simple life from my childhood. I miss the place I grew up in and my cousins and friends with whom I spent many summers playing. I miss the beautiful greenery that I woke up to each morning and tropical weather. I miss the farms where I ran around and the fresh fruits, vegetables, and meat. I miss climbing trees to get fruits. I miss the simplicity of life. Yet, when I think about home, America feels like home to me now. I have raised my children here and have spent more than half my life here. America has helped me provide a good life for my children. I came here hoping to open a world of new opportunities for my children. I worked hard for everything I have built and America has gifted me the life I live. America is my country and my home.

I Love you Even Though you are Old School, Mom!

I TOOK SMALL STEPS FOLLOWING the line ahead of me. I held my documents close to my chest as I slowly inched towards the immigration window. I checked my passport and documents again. This was the tenth time I was checking my documents in the past thirty minutes since I landed at San Francisco airport. I was scared and nervous. I was guided to the window where a white American man greeted me. The man in front of me asked me for my documents and followed it with a barrage of questions. "What is your name?" "Myra" I replied. "What is your purpose of visit to the United States of America?" and "Did you carry any food items with you on this flight?" There were several more as he browsed through my documents. I was nervous and listened intently as I formed words in response to his questions. "Welcome to the United States of America," he said as he handed my documents to me. I felt a sense of accomplishment as I walked out of the airport and into my husband's arms. We were married for six months before that day at the airport. I had traveled several miles from Philippines in dreams of starting a life with him. It was 8:30pm on a cold May night in 1997 as I walked out of the airport into the arms of the United States of America.

I walked out of the airport and felt the cold San Francisco air surround my body. I clung on to my husband for warmth. I checked my watch to see the time. It was 8:30pm and yet the sun was bright. There was daylight everywhere, which totally surprised me. I expected darkness and the moon, but was welcomed by daylight and sun. As our car drove past the tall buildings and fast cars, I realized how different my life was going to be from the sheltered life in Philippines. I was born and raised in the province in Philippines. My parents had eight daughters and I was number five on the list. While my sisters moved to Manila for school and work, I lived in the province with my family. My life in the Philippines was comfortable. My father was a government employee and worked as an accountant. He worked while my mom stayed home with us. I became an accountant because of my dad and have worked in finance for ten years now. We were eight children as I already mentioned, all girls. We went to a private Catholic school from kindergarten to tenth grade. Life was relaxed because we owned our own house. However, we weren't rich but we led a content, happy, and comfortable life. My dad made sure we had a good life, but we knew it was hard for him being the only working person. In spite of being a bigger family than our house could hold, we were extremely happy and content. I had never lived in a big city like Manila, which is why the San Francisco skyline made me nervous. It reminded me how different my life was going to be in comparison to the sheltered life I led in the Philippines. Simple everyday instances, such as sunlight at 8:30pm, reminded me of being away from home. In Philippines, my family and I prayed once the sun went down, which was around 6-6:30pm. I remember looking at my clock as the sun went down each day before getting ready to pray. Here at 8pm the sun was still bright, which surprised me to no end.

As our car drove through the city, I looked outside our car at the changing skylines. I never thought I would live in America. I remember the day my husband told me he was moving to America with his family. We were dating then. We met in high school as kids and have grown up together. He would call me every Sunday from America over the phone and we would talk for an hour, sometimes two. He worked full time while going to college at night, which enabled him to have the funds to visit me in the Philippines. He would visit home a couple times a year and would spend a month with me. During all those conversations, he never introduced America to me. He never told me how his life had changed. As I sat in the car oblivious to America, I felt my life changing in those first few minutes.

I reached my husband's home, which he shared with his parents and six other siblings in a three-bedroom house. It was crowded. My sister-in-law was going off to college in a month. During that duration, my husband and I slept in the living room. We were newly married and had no privacy. After the month, my sister-in-law moved to San Francisco emptying one room, which we eventually occupied. During the first three months of my American stay, I stayed at home all day and did not work. My husband went to work during the day and at 5pm he would pick me up from home. We would then go to San Jose State University where he was studying. While he attended classes, I would sit in the library reading books. He was scared to leave me alone at home, so we did that for the first three months. During the first three months in America, I had to adjust to the American cold. When I landed in America, it was the coldest May of my life. In Philippines we had the dry season and the rainy season. The spring clothing here would be ideal for the Philippines weather. I owned one sweater in Philippines, which I brought with me when I came here. I realized the sweater I brought here did not protect me from the cold. I told my husband we had to do some sweater shopping if I have to survive living in America.

The first three months here brought a new hurdle and challenge each day. I was a new bride living with my in-laws under one roof, which proved very challenging. I had never cooked in my life until I got married. I knew how to make rice, but one cannot eat plain rice and canned food forever. I had to learn to cook. When I called my family in the Philippines, I would ask my mom and sisters for recipes. They would tell me everything from the ingredients I needed to buy to the amount I needed to add in the dish. I wrote down each step as my mother and sisters narrated the recipe to me over the phone. Each week they would give me three new recipes over the phone. I had one sister in the United States who would also give me her recipes. My life in America was very different from my life in the Philippines. In spite of being number five among my sisters, I was very protected by my parents, especially my mother. My sisters would always tease me, "You are mom's favorite child." When I returned home from work, my mother would cook for me. I remember we would have crab and my mom would not let me break the shell. She would break the shell and get the meat out for me. She did not want me to exert my hands after working all day. She knew I was tired and that I skipped my lunch sometimes at work. She always had food for me when I reached home every day. All my life my mom always had food for us when we got home from school and then work. It was cultural, too. In the Asian culture, I think all parents cook for his or her children. My earliest memory includes coming home from school and my mom telling us she had snacks while we waited for dinner. As I cooked dinner as a new bride, I missed these simple moments from my growing up years.

After three months of being here, I started interviewing for jobs. In the Philippines, the interview process was very intimidating. While language proved to be a hurdle for me in America, the interview process was not as intimidating as in the Philippines. I was confident in my skills, experience, and my knowledge as an accountant. I was always confident, but in the Philippines confidence and knowledge did not guarantee one a job. It also depended on whom you knew. As I began working as a teller at a bank in America, I noticed the work culture here was drastically different to the Philippines. In the Philippines, we worked long hours. There were days when I skipped lunch. The days when I took a lunch break, it was often at 1:30 or 2 in the afternoon. We referred to our supervisors as Madam or Sir. We normally wore dresses to work and if we decided to wear pants, it had to be trousers. Jeans were frowned upon at the workplace. As I began working here I noticed they had a specific lunch hour, which was at noon. I really liked addressing my supervisor by their name and it helped promote equality at the workplace. I also liked the liberal work environment, where one could either dress up or dress down depending on a personal choice.

During the three months when I did not work, I started reading the DMV book on driving rules in America. I had never driven a car in the Philippines. I realized pretty soon I would need to drive if I wanted to go places. Initially my father-in-law drove me everywhere. Sometimes I would take the bus to places. When I initially started working at the bank, I would take the bus to work. Sometimes I would miss the bus and be late to work. It was scary to take the bus with my communication problems. I decided I had to get my license soon. After passing my written test, I was ready for my on-road driving training. My husband decided to teach me to drive, but soon enough realized it was a bad idea. We fought the whole way. I ended up learning to drive with an instructor. I sat behind the wheel the first time and felt all the rules vanish from my memory. I could not remember the controls on the car. I did not know how to turn on the left and right indicator on the car. My brain blacked out as I sat in the car nervous and scared. I stepped on the brake several times. In spite of the driving being more streamlined in comparison to Philippines, I was scared to death. In the Philippines, they are very aggressive while driving and people tend to honk a lot at each other. They do not have designated lanes and it is mad chaos. Each time I was not driving, I reasoned with myself regarding how lucky I was driving in America and not in Philippines. I told myself to be brave, but when I got in the car nervousness crept in again.

Communication continued to be my nemesis as I started working in America. When I worked as a teller at the bank, I often had to communicate with clients. I worked at the Bank of America in Milpitas, California. While the majority of the clientele I interacted with were Asians, there were Americans who did business at our branch. In one instance a Caucasian man approached my window and asked me a question regarding his account. I explained the procedure to him, but he looked baffled. I continued explaining but the more I talked, the more confused he looked. Eventually, when I realized he was losing his patience with me, I called for my manager and asked him to talk to the client. This happened to me very often. There was one instance when I remember being very embarrassed and almost crying in front of the client. I was trying to sell him one of our services. I left the window after trying to explain the service for over thirty minutes. I had to gather my composure. For thirty minutes I tried explaining to him several times and he could not understand me. I realized later I should have used the brochures to explain it to him. Instead of speaking at length about it, I should have let the brochures do the talking. As I think about it today, it is funny, but I remember standing in front of him flushed with embarrassment and with tears in my eyes.

Time seemed to fly by as I started working at the bank. I had lived in America for a year at this point. We continued to live with my parents-in-law. It was extremely hard on me and I wanted to move out. After a year, I suggested to my husband we move out. I waited patiently, hoping each day would be the day we moved out. After waiting patiently for a year, I decided to initiate the move. I surprised my husband with the apartment application form and asked him to sign on the dotted lines. It has been eighteen years since I moved to America. I believe had I not initiated the move sixteen years back, I would still be living with my in-laws.

Two years into being in America, I gave birth to my son. As I watched him grow, I realized the years have just sped past me. He is sixteen years old now. Through these sixteen years, I have changed as a person and as a mom. I come from a conservative Catholic family in Philippines. When I was growing up in the Philippines, I had strict rules. I had to be home by 6pm. If I reached home after 6pm, my mom would be angry with me. My mom was very strict. My dad would sometimes say yes, but then my mom would say no and it was a no. My husband's family was more liberal than my family. When I had my son, I decided to imbibe some of their liberalism in me. I knew I did not want my son to feel choked by all the rules. I am not very liberal, but I try to not be too conservative either. I don't want him to rebel or fight against us. Right from an early age, I have tried to be his friend more than his mother. We have a very open relationship and we talk about everything. Sometimes my son would show me a girl's picture and ask me if I thought she was cute. I would give him my honest opinion. He once liked a girl in his school and asked her to the mall. She was Filipino like him. I think she liked my son too. When her parents found out, they banned her from going out with my son. They blocked him from her Instagram, Twitter, and other social media. My son was heartbroken after that incident. I told him he needed to move on. If they were meant to be together, things would work out. I need to balance being the mother and friend when similar situations arise. My son does not share the open relationship with his dad. My husband knows about everything because I tell him. He says it is normal.

My relationship with my son is very different from the one I had with my parents. I could never imagine talking about a boyfriend to my parents when I was sixteen. Children are very outspoken here. They express themselves very well here. When my son has an opinion, he will openly express it. I could never imagine telling my mom, "Mom, it is like this or that," about something. It would be considered disrespectful if I were to reason with them. Initially when he would disagree with something I said or expressed his opinion I would say, "Excuse me!" He would then reply, "Mom, I am just saying my opinion. I am not trying to disrespect you. I know my boundaries." The culture here is very different than what I was raised in. I remember being sixteen years old and not wearing any makeup in the Philippines. I never wore makeup back in the Philippines. Even after eighteen years in America, I continue to not wear makeup. I am very pale, so I put some blush on my cheeks. Sometimes I look in the mirror and I feel, "Oh my God, I am so red." I wipe most of my blush at that point. I am amazed at how much makeup people wear in America. Even teenagers in my son's school wear so much makeup. They have their makeup on, hair done, wearing fashionable clothes, etc. I am very impressed. I wasn't like that as a teenager. I guess it is my Catholic upbringing where you have to dress in a certain way for school. Although my son has no uniforms, I insist on him dressing a certain way. He cannot go to school in a tank top. If he wears shorts, it has to be cargo shorts. I iron his shorts for him. He cannot go to school in slippers.

Schools in America have more projects for parents than the student. My husband and I were raised in Philippines, so the school system here is alien to us. I often research for hours about the school system here. It involves Google and calling the school sometimes just to understand what is required of us. When my son has a project he tells me what he needs. I help him with everything. When he was younger, I would ask him to memorize whatever he needed to and he would then recite to me. I feel I am going to school with him. In Philippines, it does not take this much work from the parents. It drives me crazy sometimes.

When my son was born, I made a conscious decision to talk to him in our language. Philippines have one main language, namely Tagalog, and several dialects. My husband and I talk in our dialect around the house and to him. He understands our dialect, but cannot talk. I think he has difficulty expressing himself. He insists he wants to learn our dialect so he can converse with my family when we visit Philippines. He loves visiting Philippines. My family spoils him. It is limiting when you cannot speak the language. He knows our dialect, but not Tagalog. He says he wants to learn. He also loves Filipino food. When he was a kid, I would feed him mangoes when we visited Philippines if he did not like something. Mangoes in the Philippines are his favorite. I am glad he is so open to Philippines. I know my son will not live there, but I want him to know about Philippines and the culture there. I spent most of my life there and I want him to know that side of my life. We were driving around once and I told him something in our dialect. He responded by calling me old school. After few minutes he hugged me and told me, "I love you even though you are old school, Mom." His favorite line is, "I am not disrespecting you, Mom." When he gets excited, he sometimes uses words like son of a gun, but he comes back right away and apologizes. I let him share his opinions on things as long as he has good values.

My son is my only child and I am extremely protective about him. My husband does not like it, but I tell him I can't be blamed for it. I have only one. I am always watching him like a hawk. I sometimes think my son does not behave like a sixteen year old. He is physically a grown boy, but he acts like a kid. He plays like a child and is still very innocent. I sometimes think he is not matured and independent because I over-protected him all his life. I just can't help it. He is and will always be my baby. I can't see him as anything else. I try to enforce our religion at home, as well. When I was growing up, it was important to go to church every Sunday in addition to other obligations. My mom would not let us skip church. We are Catholics. My husband does not go to church here. He drops my son and me at church and waits outside. I don't understand why he has boycotted going to church.

I have lived in America for eighteen years now, and in these years I have missed my parents a lot. My parents have visited America since I lived here. My mom loves shopping in America. She likes going places here, but she does not want to live here. My parents gave up their visa and their green card. They don't want to be citizens here. We cannot force them to come here, so my sisters and I visit them back home. I remember the first time my parents came to visit us. My parents visited my sister in New Jersey in 2005. I am not sure what my father felt, but he decided to leave my mother behind and visit me in California. Soon after he went back to the Philippines and passed away from cancer. I remember receiving the call from my sister. I was trembling hearing about his death. The distance makes dealing with it harder. We tried to buy tickets to go back in all the chaos. I felt helpless as I almost watched my family deal with his death. I was far away and by the time I reached home it was already days. The distance seemed real at that instant when I heard my father passed away. The flight couldn't be fast enough as I traveled to see my dad for the last time. I have visited Philippines several times and have seen it improve each time. People are adapting to the western culture. There are KFC's and Burger King's in every corner and the lines outside the stores are long. People love eating in these restaurants.

It's been eighteen years since I have been living in America. I should have been used to living here, but there are still instances where I cannot find the right word while communicating and feel jitters. Even after all these years I have an accent and I don't speak American English. I continue to wear my hair short and my face with minimal to no makeup. I continue to miss my family just as much as I did when I first moved to America. There are several things I miss about Philippines. I miss the closeness of family. The lifestyle in Philippines may have become Americanized, but it continues to be very laid back. When I was living in the

Philippines, I had time to shop after I returned from work. I would be relaxed and rested by the end of it. Here I have no time for anything. I am so tired by the time I get home and I am not rested because I have chores to do after I reach home. It is very mechanical and busy here. My husband talks about moving back to the Philippines after my son is settled. I ask him how he could go back when our son will never move back. He tells me I could stay here while he lives in the Philippines. I am torn between America and the Philippines when I think about home. Philippines will always be home for me because my mom and sisters live there. My roots are from there and I have spent majority of my life there. America is home, too, because my husband and son are here. I know my son will not move to the Philippines. I cannot think about moving back because he is here. Even if he moved out of my house I would want to be close enough so I can see him once in a while. My son makes America 75% my home by living in it.

I Was Freezing in Hawaii!

I OPENED THE ENVELOPE and stared at the word "accepted". I re-read the letter several times as the chaos of being accepted to an American university echoed in my house. I have always been a topper, an achiever of accolades and merits all my life, yet this acceptance felt surreal. I had filled out several applications over months and waited with baited breath to hear back from the schools I had applied to. In spite of being a topper, I have battled uncertainties and doubts while waiting for my acceptance. The word "accepted" validated all insecurities I had battled as my dream to study in America was finally culminating into reality. I was going to attend a graduate program at the University of Hawaii in the United States of America. For this young girl from eastern China, the word accepted was a culmination of a long dream of academic excellence. The year was 2001, and I packed my bags and moved to Hawaii from China to begin my graduate studies in electrical engineering. As I boarded my first flight with my new husband, I was excited for the days ahead in America.

After a long flight ride from China to America, we landed in Hawaii. I had no idea what America would be like, but Hawaii was well documented around the world. I knew Hawaii was an island with beautiful blue waters, the place most people went on their honeymoon and a tropical paradise with warm weather. I knew Hawaii from all the advertisements and documentaries I had watched and heard about. I expected it to be warm based on my prior knowledge. Instantly, I realized it was not as hot as I expected it to be. It was colder than I prepared myself for. The air conditioner at every indoor location proved to be a major hurdle for me. It was 90 degrees outside and 60 degrees indoors, which proved challenging for dressing. Do I dress in shorts and t-shirt or do I bundle up for the cold inside? Outside I often saw people dressed in shorts, t-shirts, and sandals. I bundled myself with a coat, which I am sure looked weird to the locals. I was freezing in Hawaii.

My husband and I were accepted to the university, which made the initial days in an American university easy for me. Although we were both studying different majors, having him on campus was comforting. On our very first day in college, I went to the cafeteria and asked for some water. They handed me ice water. I was already freezing from the air conditioning, and this cup of cold water froze me further. I asked for some hot water. Every time I went looking for hot water in the cafeteria, people wondered why I was looking for hot water in an already warm Hawaii. They did not know I was freezing inside.

I came to America to study electrical engineering. I already had my undergraduate degree in electrical engineering from China. I was born and raised in eastern China in a small, quaint town. When you say China in America, people instantly think about Beijing and big cities like Shanghai. My town in eastern China was smaller in comparison to Beijing and Shanghai. I had a very simple upbringing being an only child to my parents. Family always surrounded me. I was always shy and introverted. At an early age I was sent away to one of the bigger cities to attend college. College life was stressful back in China. I was in a special program where I did more than one degree. I sometimes took sixty units and it was difficult. I was always stressed out during my undergraduate studies. I was prepared for a similar college experience here, but as I started taking classes in University of Hawaii, I noticed it was not as stressful as in China. I am not sure if it was because I was doing graduate studies versus undergraduate. Most of my classes were focused on projects and they were very hands on. I also had to give presentations in my classes during projects, which proved extremely challenging for me. I was introverted and shy as a person and found it challenging to converse in English.

Communication was one of my biggest challenges in America. When I first came here, I was talking to the bank clerk regarding the process of starting an account over the telephone. I could not understand anything she told me. I asked her to repeat the process over and over again, and with each instance that I made her repeat I realized I was sweating profusely. With every slang and American word she used to explain, I sat there dripping with sweat and clueless. During one of my classes, I was explaining something to my professor and stopped mid-way. He stared at me and looked confused. He had no idea why I had stopped talking mid-way through the explanation. After moments of awkward silence, he asked me, "Why don't you finish your sentence?" I told him I thought I said enough because it is stupid if I have to finish my sentence when it is so obvious. He looked extremely confused and annoyed from that situation. When my professor asked me why I did not finish my sentence, it reminded me of the several times people have been confused by my explanation or lack of in America. In Chinese communication, although it is not specified, people tend to say the first half of the sentence and omit the second half. People know what you are implying which they often demonstrate using body language or gestures, and we move on to the next topic without completing the sentence. I was used to communicating in that manner. When I came to America, I realized everything had to be spelled out even when it was obvious. People get annoyed when you don't explain everything and I am sure I have driven several people crazy by my communication. I also have trouble figuring out when to talk and when to listen. Initially when a person paused while talking,

I would voice my opinion thinking they were done. I often got looks indicating I was interrupting or I was rude. Luckily, I had mostly Chinese friends in Hawaii who shared some of these quirks, which made the transition easy.

While academic life was not very stressful besides the countless time I had to present in front of a group, adapting to the American culture was challenging. In Hawaii the weather was generally warm all year round, and to compensate for the heat there were air conditioners everywhere. I often found myself wearing thick clothes to protect myself from the cold air conditioners. Imagine walking in 95-degree heat wearing thick clothes and now imagine wearing those clothes in 95-degree heat on a college campus. I am sure I looked weird. I was dressing myself for the cold libraries and classrooms I spent most of my time in. I had no choice. I could wear sandals and shorts and freeze myself off or I could wear thick clothes and look weird. I chose the latter. One of my Chinese friends was walking the campus on a warm day with an umbrella. One of the guys stopped her and asked her, "Are you a movie star? Why are you carrying an umbrella?" She was shocked. The person told her it made no sense to carry an umbrella when it wasn't raining. When she told us about it, we could not help but laugh. We knew it was an instance of cultural difference, but it was still funny that an umbrella made her a movie star in America. In China, people use umbrellas to shield themselves from the sun. They want to preserve their complexion from getting tanned and people don't like using sunscreen. Here in America, people want a tan. You rarely see Chinese back in China sun tanning on a beach.

Culturally, Chinese women wear socks with everything. It doesn't matter if the socks are short or long, or the attire you are pairing it with. It is almost cultural to wear socks. In America, people rarely wear nude socks with sandals and open toe shoes. People want to show off their perfectly pedicured toenails. In China, you do not wear shoes without socks. It is often frowned upon to go to school and work with open toe shoes and no socks. It was a huge adjustment for me when I came here. I have adjusted to it, but I am sure I raised several eyeballs when I walked around with my open toe shoes and socks. I was making a fashion statement in my Hawaiian campus! Besides wearing socks, I have also had to adjust my fashion sense to the laid back American style. In China we wore a dress anytime one felt like wearing one. During one such occasion, I dressed up because I felt like wearing a dress. I was shocked when someone asked me, "Are you going somewhere tonight? Why are you so dressed up?" I was wearing a dress, which wasn't high fashion or an evening gown. I was shocked when I was asked the occasion. In China, people wore dresses during summer time. If I feel the urge to wear a dress to someone's house or party, I wear a simple dress I typically would have worn at home in China to the event. Even then I get complimented on how good I look because they cannot say otherwise. It would be considered rude. When I wear my simple home dress to the event, I have noticed I am not violating the casual dress code.

When I first reached Hawaii for graduate school, the Chinese ethnic groups in Hawaii surprised me. Over time, I have realized their customs, traditions, and even their food are a combination of both the cultures having lived in Hawaii for so long. Chinese food that is often claimed to be authentic is not really authentic. Most of the Chinese people in Hawaii are from the southern part of China. Their food is vastly different from the food served in southern part of China. It is Americanized and different. I had never cooked food until I got married and moved to Hawaii. Initially I spent hours on the computer finding recipes to cook. During my amateur cooking days, I chanced upon a recipe for a chicken potpie that sounded easy and interesting to cook. I decided to make the dish for my husband. The recipe asked me to use a baking mix to make the dish and I had to use two cups of baking mix. I did not know the difference between baking mix and powder, so I added two cups of baking powder. The dish was cooking when my husband came home from work. He was instantly impressed by the smell and could not wait to try it. He took the first bite and said it tasted good. He degraded it to tasting weird with his second bite and the third bite had him running to the bathroom to throw up. We went through the recipe step by step, word by word carefully and realized the baking powder fiasco. I am really glad he did not end up in the emergency. After 15 years of marriage, he still takes small bites of my new dishes just to be careful. Over time I have become comfortable with cooking. The kitchen is my play toy and stress buster after a hard day at work. I enjoy cooking every day, although we do eat out a lot, too.

After five years in Hawaii, my husband and I relocated to Fremont, California. Fremont has a big Chinese population as well. I began working in California as an electrical engineer. As I began looking for a job, I was often asked why I chose to be an electrical engineer. I find that question very shocking because growing up in a small town in China, it was the natural path for me. My family was filled with engineers, doctors and professors. I grew up in China watching my uncle invent the first satellite. He was the first engineer who was leading the project of inventing the first satellite in China back in the day. He was my role model and I looked up to him. He introduced me to the world of electrical engineering. It seemed natural to choose electrical engineering. I have often had to fend off questions about being a female hardware engineer in America, which often shocks me. During one of my job interviews, the interviewer asked me why I was doing hardware. I thought that was weird. In another interview, the interviewer told me he had never seen a woman who was good at hardware. His statement shocked me and I thought it was rude. I sat there smiling because it was an interview and I am expected to smile. Had I met him in any other scenario, I would have taken him to HR for that statement. Although I have encountered these situations when I interview, the companies I chose to work at have been equal opportunity. I have never encountered these situations there.

I met my husband when we were in college in China. We were classmates, fell in love, and eventually got married. Traditionally, China had both arranged and love marriages. I don't think parents could ever tell their children to marry someone without getting to know them. I don't think that has been the case in the last thirty or forty years. Parents might help the couple meet as in suggest each other to them, but the ultimate decision is by the couple. I got married to my husband in a traditional setting in China, and lived with him for a short while before moving to America together. We both came here as students, and relied on each other for support. Years passed by as we moved from China to Hawaii and then to California. With time, we had a son, making us a family of three.

As I see my son grow up in America, I see several differences between our upbringings. I had a very simple upbringing in China. I grew up playing outside with other children, education was the top most priority and computers were not accessible until I was in high school. My son has literally been born with a computer. While some of these changes are cultural, my husband and I have consciously made some changes to the way we raise him. While growing up in China, my parents made all decisions for us. We were never asked for our opinions. Our opinions did not matter in any situation because our parents made the choice for us. I decided to raise my son differently. Whether it was the food he eats or the clothes he wears, I let him decide. I might have direction for him to follow, but I make him believe he is making the decision for his choices. From as young as six or eight months of age, options were laid out for him so he could decide his path. He has been raised to think on his own from an early age. If he decides to eat M&M, he gets to decide how many M&M's he is going to eat considering it is junk food. I was telling my coworker how my son decided he was going to eat one M&M a day and he would eat the second one the next day because it is junk food. She was laughing wondering how he decided he wanted to eat only one, but that is how I taught him to think about things. I think this approach helps when he is disciplining himself. Sometimes it is hard to reason with him. He reasons things with me and has proof for every argument since he was three years old. It gets cumbersome to negotiate with him about everything. For now, I think this is the right thing to do.

My son speaks American English while both my husband and I were not born here. Although he has not corrected my English, I have started seeing him correct my husband's English. Just the other day he was correcting my husband as he spoke something. We laughed when he did it because we knew this day was coming. Sometimes we hear him describe worms in the garden with words we have never heard about. We ask him, "What is that again?" and as he repeats himself, one of us sneakily checks the word on our phone to see what it means. At home we speak in Mandarin with him. I am not sure how this happened, but at some point he realized we spoke Mandarin at home and English outside the house. He made the distinction when he was in preschool. He started going to school when he was 18 months old. Initially we sent him to a Chinese speaking day care. At two years of age, we sent him to preschool. He did not know any English when he went to preschool. We had an emergency English training at home where we taught him essential words like water, potty, etc. At the end of the first day he had learned five new words like thank you, please, etc.

At home, we follow our version of Chinese traditions. I imagine American families follow different traditions than us. We did not enforce our culture on him. It wasn't like he wanted to follow something else and we put our foot down saying you are going follow this. We have always maintained our Chinese culture and traditions, which are different from the American traditions. I am sure it is different than what is traditionally followed in China. My family continues to live in China. Although my family visits us in America, the language barrier makes it challenging for them. Since we moved to Fremont, it has been easier for them because there is a dominant Chinese population in Fremont. We took our son to China few years back. I have heard of people packing American foods like macaroni and cheese for children when they travel back to their countries. He was open to the food in China, having grown up on our version of Chinese food, which is a combination of American and Chinese food.

China has changed a lot over the years. Last time I visited China, everything looked so different I could not recognize anything. My son was very young when we took him back to China. He was scared of the road conditions, which were very different from here. Something as simple as people crossing the streets and cars honking scared him. Some streets were nice and well laid out while the others were chaotic, which really bothered him. When we were in China, my family organized a party for us in a restaurant. There were about sixteen people who were all seated around a big table with several dishes. During the party, I glanced at my son who seemed very intimidated by everything. He was flustered and did not seem like himself. I realized this setting was a culture shock for him. During parties in America, people tend to split up in small groups. You rarely see this many people together around a table. My husband and I did not realize it would be a culture shock. It was normal for us having grown up in China.

It has been fifteen years since I left China for Hawaii with my husband. We did not know where this journey would take us beyond the University of Hawaii campus. Today as I watch my son play around me,

I am amazed at the beautiful family I have built here. Yet, I know America has not changed the shy and introverted girl from China who boarded a flight with her husband. Even after years of living in America, I still have trouble making friends. Presentations continue to challenge me as I find it difficult to find the right words to express my intentions. Even after years I feel the jitters I felt when I first had to present in front of people. I have lived in America for fifteen years, and yet I continue to be the outsider at the party. I still have problems communicating in America. Although I can speak English, timing on when to speak has always eluded me. It somehow seems harder than it needs to be.

I have visited China several times since I left there fifteen years back. Through the years I have seen China change and today I can hardly recognize the place I grew up in. There have been several differences from zoning and landscaping of the cities. People have been constantly moving around because of these urbanization changes. My family has moved along the way, too. When I visited China with my family few years back, everything looked different. I could not recognize the streets I grew up on, the house I called home did not exist anymore, and the landscaping was different. I did not recognize the China I had visited. I felt disconnected to the place I was born in. It has been this way my entire life. I have always moved around, sometimes because my family was moving and later because of college. I have never been able to establish an emotional connection to China in spite of growing up there. Despite not having an emotional connection, there are several aspects of China that I miss dearly. I miss having family around, which has always been a big aspect of my life growing up. I miss speaking in Mandarin. I miss being able to communicate freely. I am fluent in Mandarin and have authored several published works. I miss the comfort of speaking my language. No matter how comfortable or fluent I might be in English, Mandarin is still my native language. It is an integral part of the person I am, my upbringing, and the country I have called home growing up. I have been living in California for 10 years now, possibly the longest I have lived in any place in my entire life. I feel a connection to California, which I have never felt in China. I have my family here, my husband and my son. This is my tree that I have grown and I am the gardener of that tree. The tree called my family makes California home.

I Married My Wife's Picture!

Since I can remember, America has always loomed over my head. Everyone I knew talked about visiting America. Everyone and their mother wanted a piece of America. I guess in some ways I wanted to be part of that crowd. It finally happened when I was a teenager. I was attending school when my dad told me he was sending someone to pick us up from school. "Where are we going, Daddy?" I asked him. Daddy said, "You are going to get your passports made." "Why?" I asked him. "You are going to America," Daddy said. I was excited and could not believe my ears. It was finally happening, although I wasn't sure what going to America meant. I wasn't sure if it was a vacation or a more permanent move. I did not know if Daddy was going to accompany us. Would I ever return to Ghana - questions engulfed my brain as I wondered how my life was going to change. Until that day in 1987, Ghana was all I knew. Although I was excited to come to America, I had questions.

Ghana is located in West Africa to the north of the equator. Hence, the weather is warm and tropical year round. We have two seasons, namely the wet and dry season. My life in Ghana was very simple, yet it was fun. I spent most of my days going to school and playing with my friends. Although the weather was hot in Ghana, we stayed close to the water, which gave us the much-needed breeze. My family was from Fante, which was up in the mountains. The weather was fifteen to twenty degrees lower in Fante than in the city where we grew up. My earliest memories of Fante include spending all my summer vacations up in the mountains. I was the oldest of twelve children. Initially I thought my parents were trying for a second boy after me. I realized it wasn't the reason when my parents continued having children even after my brother was born. My parents were from two different tribes. There are several tribes in Ghana. The Akan tribe, which is the main tribe in Ghana, has several sub-tribes such as Asante, Akuapem and Akyem, Agona, Kwahu, Wassa, Fante, and Brong. Each sub-tribe speaks a language ethnic to them. We grew up speaking Ga, which was my mother's language, while Twi was spoken in the main city. We knew Ga and Twi. My father spoke Fante. Life was fun until my dad sent us to America in 1987 to visit my stepmother.

I still remember the day I was preparing to visit America for the first time. I am not sure how things have changed now, but in 1987 people dressed up in suits when they visited America. I dressed in my three-piece suit for my flight ride to America. I boarded my flight from Ghana to America and realized I was hot in my three-piece suit on the flight. My sisters and I landed in Amsterdam after being on the flight for ten hours. It felt like ten hours, but if someone had said it was a day I could believe it. I remember running around Amsterdam airport with my sisters. We finally landed in JFK airport in New York. After clearing immigration, customs, and picking up our luggage, my uncle welcomed us to America and picked us up. We continued walking through the airport towards the exit. We reached a sliding door and my uncle walked through it swiftly. My sisters followed him, but at a slower pace. It was my turn to walk through the sliding doors into America. I turned around and walked myself back. My uncle stopped and asked what I was doing. I told him it was too cold. The cold January New York air pierced through my skin into my bones. I had never felt spine-numbing cold of this kind before. I remember the cold being different from anything I had ever experienced. Eventually I braved the cold and walked out of the door. We stayed in New Jersey for a month, after which we went back to Ghana.

Three years later, I moved here for good. This time when my daddy told me we were going to America, I did not feel the excitement or fear I felt the first time around. I accepted I was going to America.

My second visit to America was in 1989 or 1990. I was more prepared for the American cold having braved it the first time. I believed my previous vacation in America prepared me for this trip. I thought I wouldn't have too many shocks. However, I failed to realize I was here for more than a vacation. I was going to live here permanently this time. I started ninth grade in America. My mom dropped me off at school. I wondered why I wasn't wearing a uniform to school. I assumed it was because I did not have one yet. I reached school and noticed no one wore uniforms here. I went to the British school system in Ghana and there were rules, which were non-negotiable and had to be followed. We were not allowed to talk during class. When the teacher had to leave the classroom, she would assign one of the students to monitor the class who wrote down your name if you spoke in class. When the teacher returned, she not only punished you for talking, but would also call your parents to report your indiscipline to them. When you reached home, you were in serious trouble. I was used to this system in school. My first day in my American class I noticed the students were talking as the teacher was trying to teach. I tried to tell the student next to me he would be beaten if he did not stop, but he did not listen to me. He gave me a look and told me to shut up. I was appalled and scared. When my (step) mom picked me up that evening I told her, "Mom, I am sitting in the class and everyone was talking. The teacher was trying to talk and everyone was talking. I was so afraid. I thought we were all going to get beaten." She laughed and told me no one was going to beat me. I told her while my teacher might be nice, she will beat us if we talked during class. I did not understand why the students in my class wouldn't listen to me when I told them they would be beaten. I found that very strange.

Communication was never a problem for me because I spoke English confidently. I had problems understanding people initially. I often asked them to repeat themselves and my vocabulary always included pardon me, excuse me and sorry I did not get you. Initially, Americans seemed to talk faster than I could comprehend. I got teased for how I spoke rather than my accent. This boy in my class once asked me, "Why do you talk English so weirdly? Why don't you say what's up like the rest of us?" I was young and was trying hard to fit in. I decided to talk like the other kids in the class. However, when I first said what's up I realized it did not sound as smooth as the others. When I first started going to school, one of the kids in my class told me, "You are so dark." It did not bother me, but I never understood why he specified that. I grew up around people who were of different colors, so I never stopped and thought about my color in all my years in Ghana. Even in Ghana, people have a fascination for light skinned people who are considered attractive because they are light skinned. I think it is everywhere in the world, so it does not bother me. I however don't understand the fixation or do not comply with that ideology.

A few weeks after I landed in America, my mom bought me a Walkman. Some of the music I listened to while growing up included Michael Jackson and other mellow music. I did not know rap music beyond Grand Master Flash. I started my Walkman in school and walked around, moving to my music. One of the boys in my class stopped me and asked what I was listening to. I proudly said, "Michael." When he looked baffled, I told him, "Michael, Michael Jackson." He was shocked as he told me, "You need to listen to some real music." He handed me his rap music and told me to listen to it. He told me it was good and I should listen to it. As much as I loved Michael Jackson, I started listening to rap. I started rapping at home and used words which were not allowed in an African household. My mother warned me against using those words at home. Every time I think about my rapping days, I think they were some of the funniest days of my life. African parents expect children to be very respectful in their manners and the way they talk to older people. If you talk a certain way, it is considered rude, disrespectful, and will portray you in a bad image to others. I wasn't aware America had no such concrete rules. I was telling one of my friends at school about my life in Ghana. When my father returned home from work in Ghana, I removed his shoes being the oldest son, I told my friend. My sisters brought him water and my mom brought him the meals. I was proudly flaunting my lifestyle from back home while my friend looked shocked. "Where did you come from, man?" he asked me like I was from another planet.

As the years went by, I became more comfortable with my life in America. I finished high school and college. I might have become comfortable with America, but I still yearned to go back to Ghana. A part of me missed everything about my life there. In 2003, I made my first trip back to Ghana. I was ecstatic when I booked my tickets to go back home. It seemed like a dream come true for me as I told my friends in America I am going home. It had been over ten years by then since I had visited Ghana. After that first trip, I decided to go back every two years. And then I decided to be back every year. I planned my trips to Ghana in December and I would stay there until January. I did that every year, so either December or January of the year I was in Ghana. It gave me a solace knowing I was going back home every year. The very first time I went back, I saw several developments there. The western influence was very evident in the way people dressed up. When I was growing up in Ghana, we wore slippers, but now children wear the latest sneakers and shades. I don't remember wearing shades when I was there. Internet and social media have made it easy to emulate the western culture. The influence of hip-hop culture is very apparent there. I was shocked to see youngsters sag their pants and walk like hip hop stars. Every time

I go back, I see Ghana getting more westernized. When I visited in 2007, my cousin and I went to a nightclub. I was people watching and was shocked at what I was seeing. The women in the club were almost naked. Guys referred to their women as bitches. This was not the Ghana I grew up in. Back then if they were wearing 40% more clothing than the women were in the club, they could not have left their house. My cousin came over and asked me if I was okay. I said, yeah, I was just shocked at how people had changed. I knew this was the hip-hop influence. I wanted to tell them the hip-hop videos were selling an image. The people in those videos most likely did not act like that in their personal life.

I continued to travel to Ghana every year and work in America. I got married to my wife few years back and have a two-year-old son. My wife was born and raised in Ghana. It was always important to me I marry a girl from back home being the oldest. My family would have accepted any girl I brought home irrespective of where she was from. I know my dad would always wonder if I would never return back had my wife not been Ghanaian. We had a court wedding in America and an engagement in Ghana. As part of the Ghanaian culture, when a guy wants to marry a girl he tells her I want to get engaged/married to you. The bride will then tell her father of the guy's intention. He will give a dowry list for the groom, after which they can get married. My wife's family gave me a similar list. I looked through the list and stopped at an item that asked for a large sum of money. I re-read the item again and again. It was in my language and I was sure I read it right. I consulted my father to see if he knew what that amount was for. My father told me I was in trouble. The large sum of money was the result of my wife being pregnant before marriage. I did not have that kind of money, so she stayed back in America and I had our wedding in Ghana. I married her picture. It was weird walking down the aisle with a picture of my wife. She complains about how she missed the festivities and wants to do it again.

After our wedding, my son was born in America. Since he was born I have been speaking to him in our language and my wife always tells me, "He does not understand you." She always tells me that my son does not understand me. She thinks I make up stories so I can feel he understands me. One day not too long ago I was home alone with him and was playing with him. I told him to come here in our language and he came. When I told my wife she told me he didn't understand me. I told her to speak to him in our language and she refused. In another instance he said something in our language when we were both home and she refused to believe it. She repeated that he does not understand. I continued to encourage her to speak our language with him. One day at work I got a text saying, "He understands." She was home with him and was speaking in our language. He reciprocated and said something back. She is a believer now. My son is pretty smart I think and is very tricky guy. When we speak to him in our language, he pretends he does not understand and when we talk to him in English, he has a what-are-you-saying look on his face.

My daddy always told us we should speak to our children in our language from birth, so they can understand the language. He believes they will eventually learn to speak the language if they can understand it. My sister always shrugged it off, too. When I asked her if she spoke the language with her kid, she said, "Nah." Two weeks back I received a text from her startled by her child. Her husband was in the kitchen doing something while their kid was shaking the gate separating the kitchen from the other room. He kept saying stop and the kid continued to do it. He turned around and said stop, to which the kid said stop in our language. My sister and her husband's jaws dropped because they did not know he even spoke the language. I guess my daddy was right in telling us to speak in our language. When we go back to Ghana this December, I hope to take my son to our village so he can learn the language just like I learned the language as a child. I grew up speaking in Ga and Twi that was different from the language my father spoke. My daddy's family teased him about how his children did not know his language. We could understand the language, but could not speak it. Whenever we went for vacations, people spoke to us in Twi. This one summer when we went to Fante, my sister and I went to the store. When we spoke to the lady in Twi, she responded in Fante. We were confused why she would respond in the other language. We found out my daddy had asked everyone to speak to us in Fante when we spoke in Twi. This happened every time we went to Fante. Over time, just by interaction, we began understanding them. So I plan to do the same with my son.

When I came to America and was on my own, I had no one to speak in Fante. Most Ghanaians I met knew Twi and did not know Fante. I retained Twi. Now when I visit Fante, I am teased about not knowing the language. I am the first-born, too, so it is embarrassing. My uncle got married recently. His wife speaks Ga and does not speak Twi. I knew his wife since we were young. I always told her to learn Twi and she refused. Now when my uncle wants to talk about her, he switches language on her. He gets excited he can talk about her without her understanding it. Whenever I visit them and explain Twi to her, he gets upset. My ex was Kenyan and every time we were around my family, we spoke in our language. We would come home and fight about it. She would tell me, "You know I am there it is rude." I can't tell my mom not to speak our language. Some of us, including myself, mix English with our language so it makes it easier to understand for someone who doesn't know the language. You also feel like they are talking about you. Language is an important part of our culture.

Besides his language, we hope to work on my son's eating skills in Ghana. He is a slow eater, which I originally did not think much about. The other day I grilled corn on the cob, which happens to be his favorite.

I gave him a corn on the cob and he was nibbling slowly on it. I took a bite off of his as he was eating. Next thing I know, my slow eating son was chewing the life out of the corn. I realized he could eat fast when there is competition. In Ghana he would share food with his cousins in a pot. He will realize he would have to eat fast, else the food will disappear. I think that would speed up his eating. We cook Ghanaian food at home. My wife is obsessed with spice. Sometimes she makes dishes with four habaneros in her dishes. I am welcomed home by the strong pepper aroma and I know I am in trouble. While I might have trouble with the spice, my son loves it. The first time he had a spicy dish, he was looking for water, but now he is a spice junkie, too. We start them young on spice and language.

My father visits us often in America. He came here recently for my son's naming ceremony. This year we plan to visit Ghana in December. In spite of going back frequently, I often ponder about going back and living there. My father ends every phone conversation by asking when we are coming back. He wonders when I will bring my son back to Ghana for more than a visit. He wants me to send my son back to Ghana for few years. I have thought about it and I know I cannot leave him in Ghana while I am here. My wife, who I thought would hit the roof, is surprisingly fine with our son going and living in Ghana with our parents. I cannot imagine not hearing his "daddy daddy" calls and his sputtering tiny feet in our house. We are seriously considering moving back to Ghana so we can expose our culture to my son. We want him to soak in the culture, learn respecting his elders, and the language. I hope I can raise my son without the generational gap between us. When I was growing up in Ghana, there were topics I could not talk to my dad. I could never tell my dad about a girl I liked. I hope my son can tell me anything. I want him to come to his parents when he needs advice. American culture is very different from Ghana. My dream for him is to bridge American culture and Ghanaian culture so he can have the best of both worlds.

In 2007, I visited a friend to deliver some packages. I found out his brother had won the American visa lottery to come here. His mom told me he was looking for tickets. I asked him when he was planning to come. I had planned to stay in Ghana for two months during that trip. He told me he was leaving a few weeks before I was scheduled to return. The next day he came over to my house and asked me to change my tickets so we could leave together. I looked at him like he was crazy and said no way. In fact, I was hoping to stay another month if possible. He did not understand why I would not want to return back to America. After I reached America, I called him to see how he was doing. He told me I was right and it was too boring. Nobody talked to him here. He told me he walked around and said hi, but no one held a conversation with him. In Ghana, you could meet a random person and have a one-hour conversation with them. A few weeks later he called excitedly and told me," Man, I was at the bus stop and this old lady sat next to me. She said hi to me. Can you believe it we talked?" I burst out laughing! I told him he was never going to hear the end of this. He got excited because an old lady talked to him. I remember when I was growing up in Ghana, my working cousins would have their friends come over after work and they would be there for days without going home. The culture is very casual and informal which I miss dearly.

I miss Ghana and plan to move back. People think I am moving back because it is expected of me. I am moving back because I want to go back to my country. I miss the freedom in Ghana and I have always felt less stressful being there. I don't have to worry about rent or bills. We own a house there. The most important aspect of Ghana that I miss is relationships. The dynamics I share with my friends back there is different from the one I share here. This one time I was in Ghana, I had gone out with some of my friends at 10am and came back at 5pm. As I walked to my house, I saw some of my other friends who were waiting for me. I found that they had been waiting for me since 10:30am. A moment like this makes Ghana special. I miss the informal interaction with people. When I am in America my mind is thinking about a million things.

I came to America in 1990 and have lived here for a long time now. I have lived here longer than I have lived in Ghana, yet Ghana continues to be home. Initially I used to tell people I am going back home when I am visiting Ghana. When I am there, I would tell my family I am returning to America. Over time I have started referring to America as home. Ghana and America have a rivalry in soccer during the World Cup. Through the years, I have been a Ghana supporter. When my family used to call me in America to taunt me about how they were going to beat me in the world cup, I would tell them I am one of you. I am Ghanaian, too. This past World Cup I noticed I was torn between Ghana and America. I wasn't sure whom to support. When my family taunted me about beating me, I told them it was not going to happen. Over the years America has started feeling like home. My family and friends assume I am American because I live here. They don't realize I miss Ghana every day. I miss it right now as I am giving this interview. It is my roots, the country I have spent the best years of my life in, and the country I identify with the most. I carry Ghana in my heart and soul. Ghana is my home and will forever be the place I call my home.

CPSIA information can be obtained
at www.ICGtesting.com
Printed in the USA
LVHW080801310119
605583LV00007B/4/P

9 781628 655520